# THE COMMON CORE STATE STANDARDS

## for Literacy in History/ Social Studies, Science, and Technical Subjects

### FOR ENGLISH LANGUAGE LEARNERS

### Grades 6–12

LUCIANA C. DE OLIVEIRA, EDITOR

*The Common Core State Standards for English Language Learners Series*
*Luciana C. de Oliveira, Series Editor*

Typeset by Capitol Communications, LLC, Crofton, Maryland USA
and printed by Gasch Printing, LLC, Odenton, Maryland USA

TESOL Press
TESOL International Association
1925 Ballenger Avenue
Alexandria, Virginia 22314 USA
Tel 703-836-0774 • Fax 703-836-7864
www.tesol.org

Senior Manager, Publications: Myrna Jacobs
Cover Design: Kathleen Dyson
Copy Editor: Tomiko Breland

TESOL Book Publications Committee
    Robyn L. Brinks Lockwood, Chair
    Elizabeth Byleen
    Margo DelliCarpini
    Robert Freeman
    Deoksoon Kim
    Ilka Kostka
    Guofang Li
    Gilda Martinez-Alba
    Allison Rainville
    Jason Stegemoller
    Adrian J. Wurr

ISBN 9781942223665
Library of Congress Control Number 2016933664

# Contents

## Content-Area Integration

# Series Preface

The Common Core State Standards are a set of educational standards for kindergarten through 12th grade in English language arts and mathematics. These standards "are designed to ensure that students graduating from high school are prepared to enter credit bearing entry courses in two or four year college programs or enter the workforce" (National Governors Association Center for Best Practices & Council of Chief State School Officers, 2013). They specify what students in grades K–12 should know and be able to do to graduate from high school, attend and graduate from college, and participate in the global economy. The CCSS have been adopted by 45 states, the District of Columbia, four territories, and the Department of Defense Education Activity (National Governors Association Center for Best Practices & Council of Chief State School Officers, 2012).

The K–12 student population in the United States is becoming increasingly diverse. More than 15% of the K–12 student population is comprised of English Language Learners (ELLs), which represents over 5 million students in U.S. schools (National Clearinghouse on English Language Acquisition, 2012). Yet this student population is consistently ignored when content standards are conceptualized and often treated like an afterthought. This was the case with the CCSS, which were designed for a general student population and provide little guidance for teachers who have ELLs in their classrooms. The only direction given is a two-page document entitled "Application of Common Core State Standards for English Language Learners" (National Governors Association Center for Best Practices & Council of Chief State School Officers, 2010) that provides very general information about ELLs and their needs. This document does not provide any guidance for teachers in how to adapt and use the CCSS with ELLs, and nothing about how to address the demands and expectations of the standards with this student population.

Given CCSS adoption in so many parts of the country and the demographic shifts in the number of ELLs, it is imperative that teachers be prepared to address and adapt the CCSS to the language and content needs of ELLs. This book series focuses on this urgent need to provide guidance for teachers who will be implementing the CCSS in classrooms with ELLs. When I started to conceptualize this series, I immediately thought that teachers of ELLs would need to know more about some pedagogical practices that will help them focus on the CCSS with ELLs, modifying what they already do with their students without simplifying instruction. The main goals of the series are to examine the potential content and linguistic challenges of the CCSS for ELLs and describe practices, strategies, and key ideas related to supporting ELLs across the grade levels in the content areas covered by the CCSS.

The audience for the book is practicing teachers, pre-service teachers, graduate students, academics, researchers, and professional development providers. These books can be used in a variety of courses, including methods, literacy, and mathematics courses in elementary and secondary teacher education programs. The books will also be a resource for practicing teachers implementing the CCSS with ELLs and professional development providers who work with practicing teachers. The Common Core State Standards for English Language Learners series aims to

1. examine the potential content and linguistic challenges of the CCSS for ELLs in English language arts, mathematics, and literacy in science, history/social studies, and technical subjects at the specific grade level span;

2. focus on edited volumes from leading researchers and practitioners working on the CCSS and with experience in the content areas and grade levels covered by each book;

3. incorporate both applied and practitioner perspectives grounded in theoretical perspectives on the CCSS and ELLs; and

4. provide accessible practices for pre-service and practicing teachers that could be used in a variety of different teacher education programs and professional development sessions.

The CCSS for ELLs book series includes the following edited books:

- The Common Core State Standards in English Language Arts for English Language Learners: Grades K–5

- The Common Core State Standards in English Language Arts for English Language Learners: Grades 6–12

- The Common Core State Standards in Mathematics for English Language Learners: Grades K–8

- The Common Core State Standards in Mathematics for English Language Learners: High School

- The Common Core State Standards for Literacy in History/Social Studies, Science and Technical Subjects for English Language Learners: Grades 6–12

The editors of these volumes worked hard to put together informative and practical books with chapters that can be adapted to different English language proficiency levels of ELLs across grades. As series editor, I planned for every book to provide helpful insights for teachers into their current practices in ways that will help them consider the needs of ELLs in every aspect of classroom instruction as they use the CCSS.

*Luciana C. de Oliveira, Ph.D.*
*Series Editor*
*The Common Core State Standards for English Language Learners*

# Introduction

*Luciana C. de Oliveira*

The Common Core State Standards (CCSS) are a set of standards developed by the National Governors Association Center for Best Practices (NGA) and the Council of Chief State School Officers (CCSSO). These standards were developed due to a perceived need by members of these associations for a set of consistent learning goals that would be common for all students across states. The CCSS are divided into two sets: English language arts (ELA) and mathematics. The ELA standards include standards focused on literacy in the content areas: history/social studies, science, and technical subjects. These standards were developed for a general student population and did not take into consideration the demands they would present for specific populations, including special education students and English language learners (ELLs). The CCSS for literacy in history/social studies, science, and technical subjects (henceforth referred to as the CCSS for literacy in HSTS), Grades 6–12 (NGA & CCSSO, 2010, pp. 59–64), in particular, present challenges for teachers who have ELLs in their classrooms due to the CCSS demands for engaging in discussions, expressing ideas clearly and fluently, reading and writing complex texts, and using language at an advanced level.

The challenges of the CCSS for literacy in HSTS and the lack of guidance for teachers offer an opportunity for considering how to best address the needs of ELLs in the CCSS era. All teachers, including mainstream content-area teachers and ESL and bilingual specialists, can create relevant units that target the development of both content knowledge and language skills of ELLs. This volume was designed to deepen teachers' knowledge and provide instructional approaches and practices for supporting 6th-grade through 12th-grade ELLs to meet the ambitious expectations of the CCSS. The chapters in this volume provide concrete ideas for engaging ELLs in a range of intellectually rich tasks to simultaneously develop content knowledge and academic English.

In Chapter 2, "Examining Cause and Effect in Historical Texts: An Integration of Language and Content," Luciana C. de Oliveira describes a pedagogical practice that teachers can use to identify cause-and-effect relationships in the content area of history. Causality is seen as particularly important for students' understanding of historical events and literacy development. The author argues that cause and effect is not just marked between clauses through conjunctions, but it occurs within clauses, making understanding the connections between events more difficult for students to comprehend. This different way of presenting causality calls attention to how teachers can help students, particularly ELLs, to focus on language to understand content, because complex texts have long been present in history textbooks, and the ability to access them is key.

Chapter 3, "Building Historical Thinking Competencies Through Image Analysis" by Sarah Drake Brown, argues that in order to prepare ELLs to meet the demands of the CCSS for literacy in history, they need to have an introductory understanding of the demands of the discipline as a way of thinking and knowing. The author outlines a systematic method of image analysis in which practitioners can engage all students in detailed and discipline-specific source analysis in their classes on a daily basis. Building students' historical thinking competencies through image analysis has the potential to establish in ELLs a firm understanding of the central concepts and structure of the discipline of history. Once students have been steeped in the language of history, they can draw upon their established understandings of the discipline's content and linguistic challenges and be better prepared to meet textual complexity as they continue to work with primary and secondary sources.

Chapter 4, "The Past Is Only Slightly Less Murky Than the Future: Corroborating Multiple Sources From Art and History" by Rhoda Coleman and Jeff Zwiers, focuses on the development of language and thinking in history lessons with a procedure that capitalizes on the use of visual arts. The procedure provides students with a rigorous, yet scaffolded, approximation of what historians do as they analyze, interpret, and discuss different sources and perspectives around a historical event. The procedure emphasizes original interpretation of art and other sources, as well as authentic communication between students. The authors place special emphasis on the activities and scaffolding that build language and serve the needs of ELLs.

In Chapter 5, "Engaging in Phenomena From Project-Based Learning in a Place-Based Context in Science," Okhee Lee and Emily Miller address the CCSS for literacy in science and highlight three key ideas. First, they discuss how the CCSS, interwoven with the Next Generation Science Standards (NGSS Lead States, 2013), present learning opportunities and demands in both language and science for ELLs in Grades 6–12. Second, they discuss specific demands as well as opportunities that ELLs may experience as they engage in argumentation. Third, components of project-based learning (engaging in phenomena) with place-based learning are presented as a pedagogical practice in which teachers and students work on various tasks that address language and content demands.

In Chapter 6, "Writing to Achieve the Common Core State Standards in Science for ELLs," Kristen Campbell Wilcox and Fang Yu suggest recommendations for writing instruction practice in secondary science classrooms. The authors focus on writing as research that has highlighted the strong correlations between writing and content learning. They discuss multimodal, project-based, and interactive instruction that addresses the use of multimodal resources, project-based writing activities, and explicit instruction balanced with dyadic and triadic interactional strategies. The authors offer examples of the practices and artifacts that they identified in their study of schools with particularly effective instructional practices with regard to disciplinary writing.

Chapter 7, "Guided Visualization: Promoting ELL Science Literacies Through Images" by Alandeom W. Oliveira and Molly H. Weinburgh, argues that guided visualization can provide science teachers with an effective means to promote ELLs' science literacies through images, and thus meet the visual demands of the CCSS. The authors demonstrate how visual decoding of increasingly complex science visuals can provide ELLs with conceptual understandings needed to perform image-to-word transformations, whereas teacher-led visual encoding can provide ELLs with the specialized language necessary to transform science texts into metaphoric visuals. Guided visualization can serve as a powerful pedagogical tool that teachers can use to promote ELLs' "representational competence" and inscription literacy regardless of linguistic or cultural background.

In Chapter 8, "Reader-Culture-Text Mergence: Seven Pedagogical Principles," Ann M. Johns argues that teachers must create pedagogies that build bridges between the text requirements of the CCSS and the needs, backgrounds, and experiences of students. This "bridges" approach to classroom pedagogy is called reader-culture-text mergence. The purpose of this approach is to narrow the gap between the within-the-text focus of the CCSS across the content areas and the life experiences of the ELLs. Johns outlines the general principles that pursue this goal.

In Chapter 9, "Writing Arguments in World Languages: Scaffolding Content and Language Learning Simultaneously," Pamela Spycher and Thierry Spycher address the use of the CCSS in integrated world language/social studies for ELLs and other culturally diverse learners in secondary settings. The authors discuss how the CCSS, integrated with the World Language Content Standards (WLCS) for California Schools (California Department of Education, 2010), present learning opportunities and demands in language, disciplinary literacy, and social studies content for ELLs and other linguistically diverse learners in high school. The authors also focus on the rationale for deciding how to meet the demands and enhance the potential of the CCSS and WLCS and provide the pedagogical practice of the teaching and learning cycle that supports students' achievement of the CCSS and WLCS while also addressing English language development standards.

Several themes weave these chapters together. One is attention to language development as a key aspect of CCSS-based instruction for ELLs. ELLs need to engage meaningfully with texts to develop their academic language and literacy skills. Developing academic language within classroom contexts is another key theme for ELLs to be successful in schools. These two themes are interconnected throughout the volume. In order for ELLs to learn academic language, they must learn it in the context of intellectually engaging tasks that enable them to read complex texts in history, science, and beyond.

Another key theme is multimodal literacy. Multimodal literacy learning and teaching involves understanding the different ways that each content area represents knowledge and the various meaning-making resources utilized in this representation. The pedagogical practices that address the use of multiple modes—visual, linguistic, gestural—provide ways of talking with students about how a variety of resources are used in the content areas. Second language learning is optimal when attention to specific aspects of language such as vocabulary, syntax, text structure, and organization work with other modalities as well as the interaction and integration of these modalities in constructing literacy in subject matter.

The chapters in this volume provide ideas for teachers to meet the high expectations of the CCSS for literacy in the content areas. These ideas highlight literacy and language education. I hope this book, along with the other books in this series, offer teachers opportunities to engage in deep conversations about what best practices support ELLs in their classrooms and beyond.

## References

California Department of Education. (2010). World Language Content Standards for California Schools: Kindergarten through grade twelve. Sacramento, CA: Author. Retrieved from http://www.cde.ca.gov/be/st/ss/documents/worldlanguage2009.pdf

National Governors Association Center for Best Practices & Council of Chief State School Officers. (2010). *Common Core State Standards for English language arts & literacy in history/social studies, science, and technical subjects.* Washington, DC: Authors. Retrieved from: http://www.corestandards.org/ELA-Literacy/

NGSS Lead States. (2013). *Next Generation Science Standards: For states, by states.* Washington, DC: National Academies Press. Retrieved from http://www.nextgenscience.org/

# HISTORY AND
# SOCIAL STUDIES

# Examining Cause and Effect in Historical Texts: An Integration of Language and Content

*Luciana C. de Oliveira, University of Miami*

The content area of history provides many opportunities for students to develop a number of different skills, including reading and writing (de Oliveira, 2008; Schleppegrell & de Oliveira, 2006). Teaching reading in history is seen as a key factor for students' understanding of content (Beck & McKeown, 2002; Massey & Heafner, 2004). In particular, focusing on students' understanding of history texts can help them become better readers (Schleppegrell & de Oliveira, 2006). Understanding how texts are organized is fundamental for student comprehension of content (Alvermann & Phelps, 1998). Reading textbooks can be difficult for students, due to the way textbooks are constructed and their lack of connection between ideas and events (Beck, McKeown, & Gromoll, 1989; Beck, McKeown, Sinatra, & Loxterman, 1991). This can be particularly challenging for ELLs, who may struggle to understand connections between ideas in textbooks.

The Common Core State Standards (CCSS; National Governors Association Center for Best Practices [NGA] & Council of Chief State School Officers [CCSSO], 2010) have many expectations for literacy in the content areas, including history/social studies. The CCSS has increased literacy demands for teachers and students; these demands involve the ability to comprehend texts with high levels of complexity, to write in different text types that present information logically, and to develop oral skills to articulate ideas in a persuasive manner. The development of these literacy skills is a tall order for both teachers and students. Complex texts have long been present in history textbooks, and the ability to access them is key.

This chapter focuses specifically on one aspect of textbook language in the content area of history: cause and effect relationships. Causality in history has received special consideration over the past several years (e.g., Achugar & Schleppegrell, 2005; Ciardello, 2002; Coffin, 1997, 2006; Unsworth, 1999; Veel & Coffin, 1996) and is seen as particularly important for students' understanding of historical events and literacy development. This chapter describes a pedagogical practice that teachers can use to identify cause-effect. Cause-effect is not just marked between clauses through conjunctions, but it occurs within clauses, making understanding the connections between events more difficult for students to comprehend. This challenge to student comprehension calls attention to how teachers can help students, particularly ELLs, to focus on language to understand content.

## The Common Core State Standards and Specific Demands for ELLs

Secondary teachers must understand the discipline-specific language demands of their content— or disciplinary language—and plan to address these demands in their classes. Within the CCSS, students are expected to engage with complex texts. In history, this complexity is often seen through the use of specific language features. When facts are organized, explained, and generalized, the discourse of history textbooks dissociates actors from actions with the construction of "things" through the use of nominalization. Nominalization is the expression as a noun or nominal group of what would in everyday language be presented as a verb, an adjective, or a conjunction. For instance, in the sentence "The violence was the people's retaliation for years of exploitation" presents two nominalizations: "people's retaliation" and "years of exploitation," which would in more everyday language be used as "the people retaliated because they were exploited for years." Nominalization is a resource used in many academic and scientific genres (de Oliveira, 2010; Schleppegrell, 2004; Unsworth, 1999) and is typical of academic discourse. Nominalizations add to the complexity of the disciplinary language of history.

Cause-effect relationships are another demand of the history content area. Causes and effects in history are constructed through a variety of language resources, not just conjunctions such as *because* and *so* (Achugar & Schleppegrell, 2005; Martin, 2002). These language resources include nouns such as *reason*, *factor*, and *result*; verbs such as *cause*, *make*, *affect*, and *lead to*; and prepositions such as *for* and *through* (Coffin, 2004; Veel & Coffin, 1996).

The CCSS have specific standards that require students to develop knowledge of cause-effect in history. The CCSS Reading Standards for Literacy in History/Social Studies 6–12 (NGA & CCSSO, 2010) state: "Describe how a text presents information (e.g., sequentially, comparatively, causally)" (RH.6–8.5; p. 61). This involves knowledge of cause-effect relationships in contrast to sequences and comparisons. For Grades 9–10, one of the expectations states, "Analyze how a text uses structure to emphasize key points or advance an explanation or analysis" (RH.9–10.5; p. 61). This involves an even higher linguistic demand to understand key points and information, often presented through causes and effects. For Grades 11–12, students are expected to "Analyze in detail how a complex primary source is structured, including how key sentences, paragraphs, and larger portions of the text contribute to the whole" (RH.11–12.5; p. 61). As students move through the grades, the demands for understanding cause-effect increase.

# Rationale

Cause-effect relationships are an essential part of history learning (Achugar & Schleppegrell, 2005; Ciardello, 2002; Coffin, 2006). Asking students to find cause-effect in history passages and draw diagrams that show cause-effect relationships is a common task found in textbooks (e.g., Beck, Black, Krieger, Naylor, & Shabaka, 2003; Deverell & White, 2006; Stuckey & Salvucci, 2003). Students are not often provided with an approach to focus on language in order to find cause-effect relationships. The approach presented here draws on a functional linguistic framework, which supports the notion that content and language cannot be separated (de Oliveira, 2008, 2010; de Oliveira, Klassen, & Maune, 2015; Schleppegrell, 2004). Content knowledge cannot be separated from the language through which it is presented, so a focus on content *means* a focus on language.

Entire clauses can also function as causes and effects, making it particularly difficult for students to recognize them (de Oliveira, 2010). Students can more easily identify conjunctions that show cause-effect, but they are less able to identify other ways that express cause-effect (Achugar & Schleppegrell, 2005). This can be especially challenging for ELLs.

Next, the pedagogical practice shows how an examination of cause-effect relationships in historical texts provides a way for teachers to engage students in talking about historical events while focusing on reading comprehension and developing literacy skills. I use an 11th-grade sample text to show the different language resources used to construct cause-effect in history. In addition, I demonstrate that recognizing cause-effect relationships helps readers understand how events are related and the reasons why they occurred, and show how cause-effect charts can be used in history classrooms.

## Pedagogical Practice: An Integration of Language and Content in Examining Cause and Effect in Historical Texts

Before we go into the pedagogical practice itself, it is important to establish an application framework that teachers can use in order to do this in the classroom. Figure 1 describes how teachers can incorporate this close look at causes and effects into their teaching.

### 1. Set goals, based on key concepts

History/social studies teachers need to set goals for the unit based on key concepts that they need to address. Typically, states have their own social studies content standards that teachers can use to select the key concepts they need to address. Teachers also need to consider and incorporate the CCSS for literacy in history/social studies.

### 2. Select a text

Next, it will be important for teachers to select a text: one to two paragraphs that address their goals and key concepts based on the standards. This text will contain key historical information and, for the purposes of this pedagogical practice, also show cause-effect relationships.

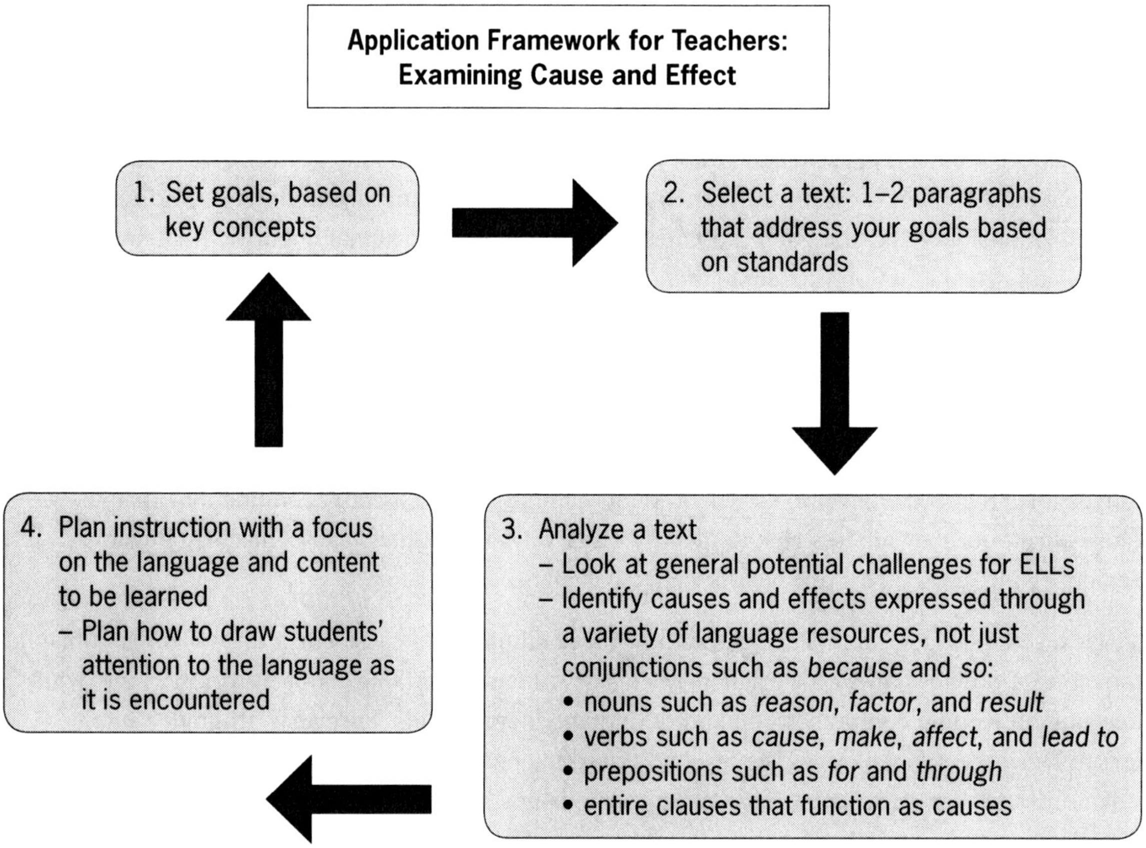

**Application Framework for Teachers: Examining Cause and Effect**

1. Set goals, based on key concepts

2. Select a text: 1–2 paragraphs that address your goals based on standards

4. Plan instruction with a focus on the language and content to be learned
   – Plan how to draw students' attention to the language as it is encountered

3. Analyze a text
   – Look at general potential challenges for ELLs
   – Identify causes and effects expressed through a variety of language resources, not just conjunctions such as *because* and *so*:
   • nouns such as *reason, factor,* and *result*
   • verbs such as *cause, make, affect,* and *lead to*
   • prepositions such as *for* and *through*
   • entire clauses that function as causes

*Figure 1. Application Framework for Teachers: Examining Cause and Effect*

### 3. Analyze a text

Next, teachers can look closely at the text. First, they can look at potential challenges for ELLs, in general. Then, they can identify causes and effects expressed through a variety of language resources, not just conjunctions such as *because* and *so*:

- nouns such as *reason, factor,* and *result*;

- verbs such as *cause, make, affect,* and *lead to*;

- prepositions such as *for* and *through*; and

- entire clauses that function as causes.

Below, I show an example of what this analysis might look like, and an activity that can help students make sense of cause-effect relationships in the text.

### 4. Plan instruction with a focus on the language and content to be learned

Next is planning how teachers will draw students' attention to the language as it is encountered in the text. This close attention to language—and, in this case, cause-effect—enables students to more closely attend to how the text presents information and is structured, as the CCSS require.

## Example of Text Analysis

The text selected shows examples of a number of different resources that construe cause-effect relationships. Examining a text by looking at causes and effects means looking for relationships between events or actions and recognizing how one event or action brought about or led to other events or actions. This is done through a close look at language.

*Sample Text* (from Cayton, Perry, Reed, & Winkler, 2000, p. 217)

---

From Farms to Cities

Women and men alike took part in the migration from rural to urban America. As factories produced more of the goods that farm women had once made, the need for women's labor on farms declined. In addition, as new machines replaced manual labor on many farms, the need for male farmhands shrank. The result was a striking shift in the nation's population. Between 1880 and 1910, the percentage of the nation's population living on farms fell from 72 to 54 percent.

Many African Americans took part in this internal migration. In 1870 fewer than a half million of the nation's 5 million African Americans lived outside of the South. But after Reconstruction ended in 1877, segregation and acts of racial violence against African Americans increased. By 1890, partly as a result of these pressures, another 150,000 black southerners had left the South, and many rural African Americans had moved into nearby cities. Then, in the 1910s, the boll weevil destroyed cotton crops and floods ruined Alabama and Mississippi farmlands. These disasters drove several hundred thousand more African Americans out of the South, mostly to Northern cities.

---

This text is an example of a *historical account* genre, where a chain of causes-effects is presented through a linear explanation of a sequence of events over time (Coffin, 2004). Several time markers are present in the text: "Between 1880 and 1910," "in 1870," "in 1877," "by 1890," "in the 1910s," and "between 1865 and 1900." Moving from clause to clause in this text can help us identify all of the cause-effect relationships presented.

The first sentence in this text ("Women and men alike took part in the migration from rural to urban America") represents what is commonly known as a topic sentence, presenting the main idea developed throughout the paragraph. The first cause appears in the second sentence: "As factories produced more of the goods that farm women had once made, the need for women's labor on farms declined." The first clause in this sentence, introduced by the connector *as*, presents the cause in the cause-effect relationship. The effect appears in the second clause, "the need for women's labor on farms declined." This cause-effect relationship focuses on *women*, introduced in the topic sentence. The second sentence ("In addition, as new machines replaced manual labor on many farms, the need for male farmhands shrank") presents further information and is constructed in the same cause-effect pattern, with connector *as* introducing the cause ("as new machines replaced manual labor on many farms") followed by the effect ("the need for male farmhands shrank"). Here the focus of the cause-effect relationship is *men*, also introduced in the topic sentence. The effect also has the same grammatical pattern: *the need for* + noun + verb. These two cause-effect sequences led to the effect, introduced by the noun *the result*, presented in the next sentence: "The result was a striking shift in the nation's population." The *striking shift* is further elaborated by the last sentence of the paragraph ("Between 1880 and 1910, the percentage of the nation's population living on farms fell from 72 to 54 percent"), which is in itself an effect of the migration introduced in the topic sentence of the paragraph.

The second paragraph focuses on African Americans' migration. The first two sentences ("Many African Americans took part in this internal migration. In 1870 fewer than a half million of the nation's 5 million African Americans lived outside of the South") provide detail about African Americans. The third sentence shows a cause-effect relationship ("But after Reconstruction ended in 1877, segregation and acts of racial violence against African Americans increased"). The first clause ("But after Reconstruction ended in 1877") can be considered a cause for the second clause ("segregation and acts of racial violence against African Americans increased"). The fourth sentence is more complex and difficult to understand due to its grammatical construction. The phrase "partly as a result of these pressures" presents the cause for two effects: "By 1890 . . . another 150,000 black southerners had left the South, and many rural African Americans had moved into nearby cities." The cause "partly as a result of these pressures" is difficult because it has the connector *as a result of* and the noun *these pressures*. The word *result* in "as a result of" may confuse students, who may think that this connector is describing an effect when in fact it is introducing a cause. The noun *these pressures* is also confusing because it refers back to "segregation" and "acts of racial violence against African Americans" presented in the previous sentence. Students may not make these connections when reading this passage.

The next sentence presents other complex cause-effect relationships. In "the boll weevil destroyed cotton crops and floods ruined Alabama and Mississippi farmlands," we find two embedded cause-effect relationships. "The boll weevil" is the cause for the effect presented through the verb *destroyed*. In other words, the boll weevil was the cause for the destruction of cotton crops. Similarly, the noun *floods* was the cause for the effect presented through the verb *ruined*. It was the floods that caused the ruin of Alabama and Mississippi farmlands. Embedded cause-effect relationships are used here to refer to cause-effect sequences that occur within the same clause such as the two clauses presented above. See Figure 2 for a visual representation of embedded cause-effect relationships.

The last sentence of the paragraph ("These disasters drove several hundred thousand more African Americans out of the South, mostly to Northern cities") marks the effect of the destruction of cotton crops and ruin of Alabama and Mississippi farmlands. The noun *these disasters*, with the

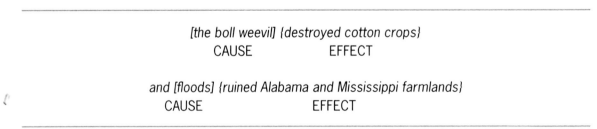

Figure 2. Visual Representation of Embedded Cause and Effect Relationships

same function as *these pressures* from the previous paragraph, refers back to what had just been presented. This last sentence also presents a cause-effect relationship: *these disasters* is the cause for the departure of several hundred thousand more African Americans from the south. The verb *drove* marks the effect: "drove several hundred thousand more African Americans out of the South, mostly to Northern cities." Again, we see an embedded cause-effect relationship, one that occurs within the same clause.

It is important to point out that the connection between what happened to cotton crops and farmlands and the departure of more African Americans may not be clear for students when they read this text. Students may not understand why the destruction of cotton crops and the ruin of farmlands affected African Americans. Teachers would need to help students make the connection, as the text assumes that students will have the background knowledge to understand how these events are connected.

Examining cause-effect relationships helps to recognize connections between events or actions and realize how one event brought about or led to other events. As can be seen, this text shows examples of a number of different resources that construe cause-effect relationships. Cause-effect is not just shown between clauses but can also occur embedded within the same clause. This can be particularly difficult for students who are unfamiliar with the language of history, especially students in the process of learning English. Teachers can help students notice cause-effect relationships by looking closely at language before students are asked to complete a diagram or discuss the causes-effects presented in a textbook chapter.

## A Focus on Language *and* History: Using Cause and Effect Charts

A close focus on language can help teachers and students recognize relationships presented in history texts. One strategy that works well in the classroom is helping students deconstruct the text through the use of cause-effect charts. I have noticed through my observation of a number of history classes that students can more easily discuss cause-effect when they deconstruct a text by looking at causes-effects in different paragraphs and then completing cause-effect charts. This helps students see the connections between and within clauses and notice the events or actions that led to other events and actions. Students find it interesting to see that most of the time, not just one event led to another event but several events are interconnected. This helps students see that history is not a series of unrelated pieces of content, but an integrated network of related content.

The sample cause-effect chart shown in Figure 3 is an example of what teachers can develop to help students see the cause-effect patterns in history texts. The chart presents the textual information in such a way to make it easier for students to realize what the causes-effects are in the text. This type of chart can be a good bridge between the language analysis and the historical questions that teachers can ask about the text. Some sample historical questions are presented below:

**Sample Historical Questions**
1. What changes happened on farms that led to a decrease in the need for women's and men's labor?

2. Why were these changes significant?

**Directions:** Fill in the following chart to see how the authors show a cause-effect pattern in these paragraphs. Some boxes are done for you.

**Remember:**

- The arrow shows how an effect can also become a cause, so repeat the text between connected boxes.
- Sometimes whole sentences can be considered causes for a certain effect.
- If a sentence is just explaining an event or providing further information, it is placed in the chart as it appears in the text (no cause-effect relationship is shown).
- In completing the chart, underline the causal expressions in the sentences.

| Event/Action as Cause | Effect |
|---|---|
| Women and men alike took part in the migration from rural to urban America. | |
| | the need for women's labor on farms declined. |
| as new machines replaced manual labor on many farms, | |
| 1.<br><br>2. | The result was a striking shift in the nation's population. |
| The result was a striking shift in the nation's population. | |
| Many African Americans took part in this internal migration. In 1870 fewer than a half million of the nation's 5 million African Americans lived outside of the South. | |
| But after Reconstruction ended in 1877, | |
| | 1. another 150,000 black southerners had left the South, and<br>2. many rural African Americans had moved into nearby cities. |
| Then, in the 1910s, the boll weevil | |
| and floods | |
| These disasters | |

*Figure 3. Sample Cause and Effect Chart*

3. The text mentions that there was a "striking shift" in the nation's population. What was this "shift"?

4. What were the causes for African Americans' move out of the south?

As students complete the chart, teachers can have them focus on historical questions that will get at the main causes and effects presented in the text. The idea here is to provide both a focus on the language and the content, so providing specific historical questions that will accompany the cause-effect charts is especially important. This text provides many opportunities for teachers and students to discuss cause-effect relationships and how they are constructed in history texts. The idea behind this close look at language is to help students understand the content presented in textbooks.

## Conclusion

Teachers and students are not always provided opportunities to consider the way language is used in their textbooks. Focusing specifically on one aspect of language in history, this chapter examined cause-effect relationships and how they are presented in a sample history text.

ELLs need to engage in causal reasoning and to recognize causal connections, fundamental aspects for history learning and understanding in the CCSS for literacy in history/social studies. Therefore, cause-effect patterns are important for student understanding of historical content. Textbooks often tell students to find markers of cause-effect, such as conjunctions, which are usually explicit in texts. Finding embedded causes and effects can help students get more meaning out of the texts they read.

As history texts are constructed in ways that may not make explicit the connection between ideas and events, it is important for teachers to be attentive to how they can deconstruct texts to help ELLs make sense of historical content. Teachers can engage ELLs in powerful conversations about the meanings presented in texts. An approach that focuses on both language and content can enable teachers and ELLs to focus on both reading *and* social studies to facilitate language development and content understanding, and address the demands presented by the CCSS.

## Reflection Questions and Action Plans

### Reflection Questions

1.  How are causes-effects presented in your textbook or other materials you use?

2.  How does working on causality in history help your ELLs learn both language and content?

3.  What language and content demands do the CCSS for literacy in history/social studies present for ELLs?

4.  What other strategies have you used to focus on cause-effect with your ELLs?

### Action Plans

*   Select a text that presents challenges for ELLs. Plan instruction to address these challenges.

*   Use the application framework presented in this chapter to examine a text that has causes-effects. Note that this same application framework can be used to identify other challenges for ELLs and other ways that a text uses other language resources.

*   Consider different ways you can help ELLs see that history is not a series of unrelated pieces of content but an integrated network of related content.

# References

Achugar, M., & Schleppegrell, M. (2005). Beyond connectors: The construction of *cause* in history textbooks. *Linguistics and Education, 16*(3), 298–318.

Alvermann, D. E., & Phelps, S. F. (1998). *Content reading and literacy: Succeeding in today's diverse classrooms* (2nd ed.). Boston, MA: Allyn & Bacon.

Beck, I. L., & McKeown, M. G. (2002). Questioning the author: Making sense of social studies. *Educational Leadership, 59*(3), 44–47.

Beck, I. L., McKeown, M. G., & Gromoll, E. W. (1989). Learning from social studies texts. *Cognition and Instruction, 6*(2), 99–158.

Beck, I. L., McKeown, M. G., Sinatra, G. M., & Loxterman, J. A. (1991). Revising social studies text from a text-processing perspective: Evidence of improved comprehensibility. *Reading Research Quarterly, 26*(3), 252–276.

Beck, R. B., Black, L., Krieger, L. S., Naylor, P. C., & Shabaka, D. I. (2003). *Modern world history: Patterns of interaction*. Evanston, IL: McDougal Littell.

Cayton, A., Perry, E. I., Reed, L., & Winkler, A. M. (2000). *America: Pathways to the present*. Upper Saddle River, NJ: Prentice Hall.

Ciardiello, A. V. (2002). Helping adolescents understand cause/effect text structure in social studies. *The Social Studies, 93*(1), 31–36.

Coffin, C. (1997). Constructing and giving value to the past: An investigation into secondary school history. In F. Christie & J. R. Martin (Eds.), *Genres and institutions: Social processes in the workplace and school* (pp. 196–230). London, England: Cassell.

Coffin, C. (2004). Learning to write history: The role of causality. *Written Communication, 21*(3), 261–289.

Coffin, C. (2006). *Historical discourse: The language of time, cause, and evaluation*. London, England: Continuum.

de Oliveira, L. C. (2008). "History doesn't count": Challenges of teaching history in California schools. *The History Teacher, 41*(3), 363–378.

de Oliveira, L. C. (2010). Nouns in history: Packaging information, expanding explanations, and structuring reasoning. *The History Teacher, 43*(2), 191–203.

de Oliveira, L. C., Klassen, M., & Maune, M. (2015). From detailed reading to independent writing: Scaffolding instruction for ELLs through knowledge about language. In L. C. de Oliveira, M. Klassen, & M. Maune (Eds.), *The Common Core State Standards in English Language Arts for English Language Learners: Grades 6–12* (pp. 65–77). Alexandria, VA: TESOL Press.

Deverell, W., & White, D. G. (2006). *United States history: Independence to 1914*. Austin, TX: Holt, Rinehart, and Winston.

Martin, J. R. (2002). Writing history: Construing time and value in discourses of the past. In M. J. Schleppegrell & M. C. Colombi (Eds.), *Developing advanced literacy in first and second languages: Meaning with power* (pp. 87–118). Mahwah, NJ: Lawrence Erlbaum Associates.

Massey, D. D., & Heafner, T. L. (2004). Promoting reading comprehension in social studies. *Journal of Adolescent and Adult Literacy, 48*(1), 26–40.

National Governors Association Center for Best Practices & Council of Chief State School Officers. (2010). *Common Core State Standards for English language arts & literacy in history/social studies, science, and technical subjects*. Washington, DC: Authors. Retrieved from: http://www.corestandards.org/ELA-Literacy/

Schleppegrell, M. J. (2004). *The language of schooling: A functional linguistics perspective*. Mahwah, NJ: Lawrence Erlbaum Associates.

Schleppegrell, M. J., & de Oliveira, L. C. (2006). An integrated language and content approach for history teachers. *Journal of English for Academic Purposes, 5*(4), 254–268.

Stuckey, S., & Salvucci, L. K. (2003). *Call to freedom: Beginnings to 1914*. Austin, TX: Holt, Rinehart, and Winston.

Unsworth, L. (1999). Developing critical understanding of the specialized language of school science and history texts: A functional grammatical perspective. *Journal of Adolescent and Adult Literacy, 42*(7), 508–521.

Veel, R., & Coffin, C. (1996). Learning to think like an historian: The language of secondary school history. In R. Hasan & G. Williams (Eds.), *Literacy in society* (pp. 191–231). London, England: Longman.

# Building Historical Thinking Competencies Through Image Analysis

*Sarah Drake Brown, Ball State University*

## The Common Core State Standards and Specific Demands for ELLs

In an ideal history classroom, students and teachers coinvestigate the past by posing historical questions and crafting written, evidence-based interpretations that draw upon a variety of sources. In the context of the Common Core State Standards (CCSS) for English Language Arts & Literacy in History/Social Studies, Science, and Technical Subjects (National Governors Association Center for Best Practices & Council of Chief State School Officers, 2010), these ideas, in part, mean that students will:

- Integrate and evaluate multiple sources of information presented in diverse formats (e.g., visually, quantitatively, as well as in words) and media in order to address a question or solve a problem (RH.11–12.7; p. 19).

- Write arguments focused on discipline-specific content (WHST.11–12.1; p. 64).

As a way of thinking and as a way of knowing, the discipline of history has specific content and linguistic demands. These requirements challenge all students and provide opportunities for the development of complex thinking, and the demands are potentially significant for students who are learning English as an additional language. How might we best prepare ELLs to successfully meet these challenges? In other words, what does it mean to integrate and evaluate *in history*? What are multiple sources of information *in history*? What are examples of the diverse formats of these *historical* sources? And how do students write arguments that focus on the *content* in history and that address *ways of thinking and knowing in the discipline*?

Given history's text-based nature, it is challenging to separate the discipline's content from its language forms and structures. In fact, the language choices made by practitioners (historians) often seem to predetermine the story told. In order to make history accessible for ELLs, teachers must begin from the premise that history is a way of thinking and knowing (Bruner, 1960; Wineburg, 2001) and uses common words in ways that are specific to the discipline. To open the discipline up to our students, we, as teachers, need to enter the mindset of historians and provide students with the opportunity to immerse themselves in disciplinary thinking.

Grammatically a noun, *history* can also be considered a verb (Drake & Nelson, 2009). The discipline represents ideas, and it communicates an action—a way of thinking about and working with ideas using a specific methodology. Whether taken as "the stuff of daily struggle" (Schlissel, 1982/1992, p. 15), "a memory of things said and done" (Becker, 1932, p. 223), or "a river into which none can step twice" (Collingwood, 1946/1994, p. 248), history and historical thought should never be understood as mere facts about dead people or as just what happened in the past. Rather, we might think of history as the way people in the present give meaning to the past in order to better comprehend the human experience. To understand how this is done and how we might help ELLs "do history" in the context of the CCSS, we must turn to the discipline, its vocabulary, and the thinking processes of historians. In other words: What is history? What do historians do? And how do historians use language to convey ideas in ways deemed appropriate by members of the discourse community? What do the CCSS mean *in history*?

In order to prepare ELLs to meet the demands of the CCSS in history, we must ensure that they have an introductory understanding of the demands of the discipline as a way of thinking and knowing. A visual breakdown of RH.11–12.7 and WHST.11–12.1 as related to historical thinking appears in Figures 1 and 2.

History is about questions. When we study history, we often wish to figure out what happened in the past, but our understanding of what happened is rarely straightforward. Rather than asking "what" happened, the vocabulary of history often begins with "why" or "how" did something occur. In order to better understand people in space and time, historians interpret the past by giving meaning to traces left behind by individuals and groups. As referenced in the CCSS, history's "multiple sources of information," or traces from the past, are diverse, and it is important for ELLs

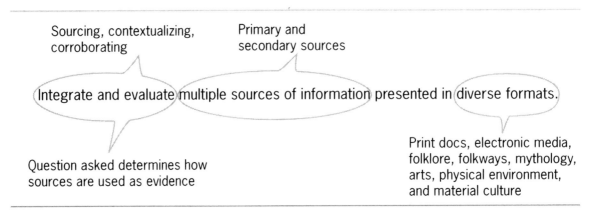

*Figure 1. Diagram of a Portion of CCSS RH.11–12.7 and What It Means in History*

For the complete typology of primary sources included as "diverse formats," see Danzer and Newman (1991).

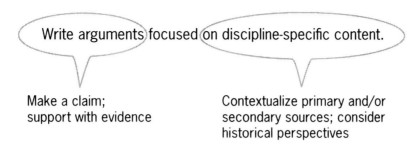

Make a claim;
support with evidence

Contextualize primary and/or
secondary sources; consider
historical perspectives

*Figure 2. Diagram of a Portion of CCSS WHST.11–12.1 and What It Means in History*

to understand how historians categorize these sources of information and how and why historians pose questions the way they do.

Historians work with primary and secondary sources, both of which present ELLs with content and linguistic demands. To meet the challenges in CCSS RH.11–12.7, ELLs need to understand why historians use multiple sources of information and what these sources are. From a purely definitional standpoint, primary sources would be those that have the first or highest rank of importance, and secondary sources would be of lesser importance. In history, that categorization works only to a certain extent. Primary sources are traces from the past that were written or created at the time period being studied. Letters, newspaper articles, music, cartoons, photographs, diaries, radio programs, television shows, articles of clothing, and countless other artifacts from the past (Danzer & Newman, 1991) can be considered primary sources. Because they are original to the time period under investigation, they are "first" in nature. Secondary sources are those that were written or created after the time period being studied and are often based on primary sources. But, because history is about questions, it is key for teachers to help students understand that whether something is considered a primary or secondary source depends on the questions that we ask. For example, Thomas J. Sugrue's book, *Sweet Land of Liberty: The Forgotten Struggle for Civil Rights in the North* (2008) is a secondary source if we are asking questions about civil rights in the 1940s. However, if we are asking questions about historians' understanding of the history of civil rights in the early 21st century, this same book is a primary source. In other words, a source becomes evidence when the source is used to answer a specific question (Seixas & Morton, 2013). Few things in history are absolute—even whether a source is primary or secondary!

As we consider the way that language is used in context, it is also key for teachers to help ELLs understand that while primary sources are valued highly due to their proximity to the period studied, secondary sources are also of great use. Secondary sources lend a valuable layer to the complex body of historical thought and should neither be disregarded nor dismissed by students. The meaning and use of primary and secondary sources in history is just one example of how the use of words must be considered within the context of the discipline and how the incorporation of "multiple sources of information" (RH.11–2.7) can present challenges to ELLs.

Integrating and evaluating sources, another component in CCSS RH.11–12.7, also requires specific ways of thinking and knowing in history. When historians evaluate sources, they often hold them up, side by side, and question the sources as a prosecuting attorney cross-examines witnesses in a courtroom (Wineburg, 2001). Specific sources are foregrounded or are placed into the background depending on the question the historian asks and the extent to which the sources contribute to the historian's argument (Lee, 2005). It is imperative that teachers help ELLs recognize that historians are interpreting—giving meaning to—sources. Because history is often construed as an argument about the past, historians must hold up various sources against each other and consider the ways in which sources can be united under specific themes or concepts to make a cohesive argument. While historians do not ignore sources that are inconvenient and they do not manufacture evidence, they do use language purposefully to craft a narrative that advances specific claims. As ELLs engage in writing arguments based on discipline-specific content (WHST.11–12.1), it is vital to teach them to consider which sources corroborate and which ones offer challenges to other sources as these artifacts from the past are used as pieces of evidence.

To provide assistance for teachers who are working with the CCSS (or similar state-created frameworks that emphasize literacy), leading organizations in academic disciplines and in social studies collaborated with state education agencies to provide voluntary guidance for states with respect to standards revision or implementation. The College, Career, and Civic Life Framework for Social Studies State Standards (hereafter the C3 Framework; National Council for the Social Studies, 2013) directs teachers toward disciplinary inquiry and emphasizes the structure and habits of mind in disciplines while also calling for application of these habits of mind through active civic life. Specific aspects of the C3 Framework that align with the CCSS and methods addressed in this chapter emphasize evidence: "Critique the usefulness of historical sources for a specific historical inquiry based on their maker, date, place of origin, intended audience, and purpose" (D2.His.11.9–12); and historical perspectives: "Analyze how historical contexts shaped and continue to shape people's perspectives" (D2.His.5.9–12).

In order to assist ELLs in building their ability to work with a variety of sources, to examine these sources as potential pieces of evidence, and to make a claim and support the claim with evidence (three stages aligned with the two CCSS introduced at the beginning of the chapter and the aspects of the C3 Framework referenced above), it is useful to incorporate images and to lead students through a systematic method of analyzing images as primary sources. By using the pedagogical practice of image analysis to promote disciplinary literacy, teachers can help ELLs first build content and linguistic knowledge that will contribute to their ability to meet the challenges of reading texts in the discipline.

## Rationale

We live in a visual culture. Given the prevalence of images in our daily lives, we are often, therefore, tempted to take students' capability in working with images for granted. Because images are "real" and seem to "show what happened," it is often cognitively difficult for students to recognize images as things that are constructed and purposeful (Gabella, 1994). Students struggle with this concept even as *they* direct friends where to stand and how to look or act in photos, deleting and retaking cell phone pictures at will because the picture "wasn't a good one." Given that students are inundated by images, it is vital that they be taught how to question these sources and to seek to determine perspective in context. These ways of thinking align directly with the CCSS outlined above and with the C3 Framework; the discipline of history provides instruction in this way of thinking, or habit of mind.

Applied linguists have drawn attention to historians' use of language to convey disciplinary concepts and construct narratives (Achugar & Schleppegrell, 2005; Coffin, 2006; Fang & Schleppegrell, 2008; Schleppegrell, Achugar, & Oteiza, 2004). Often using systemic functional linguistics (Halliday & Matthiessen, 2004), these scholars have focused on studying and improving history teachers' language awareness (de Oliveira, 2011; Fang, Sun, Chiu, & Trutschel, 2014; Schleppegrell & de Oliveira, 2006; Schleppegrell, Greer, & Taylor, 2008; Schleppegrell & O'Hallaron, 2011) and call for a language-based perspective in the content classroom. Much of this research focuses on disciplinary concepts, the writing of history, and how historians seemingly construct the content in their narratives based on the language choices they make.

Advocates of disciplinary literacy consider reading and writing to be practices best taught and most appropriately learned in the context of the discipline. They argue that because disciplinary literacy necessitates a simultaneous focus on content and on habits of mind, it follows that reading, writing, speaking, and listening processes should be taught as specialized literacy skills (Fang & Coatoam, 2013; Moje, 2008; Shanahan & Shanahan, 2008). Over the past 25 years, research in history education has documented the specialized skills in history and has noted gaps between the sophisticated thinking of historians and that of novices (Wineburg, 2001). Multiple studies of new and experienced teachers have identified various methods educators undertake to improve students' historical thinking (Monte-Sano, 2008, 2011a, 2011b; Monte-Sano & Cochran, 2009; Monte-Sano, De La Paz, & Felton, 2014a; Seixas, 1998, 1999), and researchers have built upon these studies to craft curricula designed to improve students' historical thinking competencies, often focusing specifically on teaching students to engage in historians' strategies or heuristics, specifically sourcing, contextualizing, and corroborating, as they learn to read and write in history (Monte-Sano, De La Paz, & Felton, 2014b; Reisman 2012a, 2012b; Seixas & Morton, 2013; Wineburg, Martin, & Monte-Sano, 2011).

For example, as we consider sources as evidence that bring meaning to the past, we must ask specific questions of each source. In order to help ELLs consider how or to what extent various sources can be used as evidence, it is important to ensure that they understand a central aspect of the language of history: sourcing, contextualizing, and corroborating (Wineburg, 2001). Sourcing and contextualizing involves asking specific questions of a source, and these questions need to be asked as the entry point to source analysis (see Figure 3 for examples of questions in the context of image analysis). Before trying to find out a source's main idea or determine what is happening in the source, students must consider who created the source, when it was created, the context and purpose of the creation, the worldview of the creator, and conditions prevalent at the specific place and time. In addition, they need to consider what other ideas might support (corroborate) or challenge the ideas in specific sources. Nokes (2011) suggests that when these heuristics are new to students, they receive the students' primary attention. In other words, students concentrate more on the process of sourcing the document and of asking themselves the appropriate questions than on actually doing the sourcing. Similarly, when students who struggle to analyze only one document are asked to corroborate sources, they encounter cognitive barriers. Nokes (2011) offers strategies to help students overcome these cognitive barriers when reading texts.

Reading in history does not always need a text, and images are often used as sources to help researchers study students' understanding of disciplinary concepts (Suh & Grant, 2014; Levstik,

**CORROBORATING**
What sources support the story told in the photo? What sources offer a different account?

**INTERPRETING**
How can we give meaning to the past?

**SOURCING**
When was the image taken? By whom? Where?

**CONTEXTUALIZING**
What else was happening at the same time locally? Nationally? In the world? How does this context shape the perspective of the photographer? The people photographed?

*Figure 3. Questions in the Context of Image Analysis.*

Vachon, J. (Photographer). (1941). Picket line in front of Mid-City Realty Company, South Chicago, Illinois [Photograph]. Library of Congress. Retrieved from http://www.loc.gov/pictures/item/fsa2000043792/PP/

2000; Wineburg, 2001). Studies suggest that historical thinking may become second nature for students who encounter it consistently in classroom settings (Britt & Aglinskas, 2002; Nokes, Dole, & Hacker, 2007). The emphasis on the time period prevails in sourcing and contextualizing, and this emphasis links directly to another disciplinary concept that is important when examining all sources and especially images: perspective.

As students consider the worldview of individuals and groups in different spaces and times and seek to understand historical perspectives, they encounter the challenge of presentism. Imposing present ideas or one's own values on people who lived in the past is ahistorical, but it is difficult to avoid. When seeking to understand historical perspectives, it is tempting for students to want to identify with people in the past by sympathizing with their plight or circumstances. Instead, teachers must help students exercise caution and avoid trying to apply generalizations or draw upon supposedly universal human ideas or experiences. Context is critical when seeking to determine historical perspectives, and perspective-taking relies on evidence-based inferences and ideas about the beliefs and actions of the people being studied.

Finally, ELLs must recognize the interpretive nature of history. In order to be able to read and write in history (RH.11–12.7 and WHST.11–12.1), students must recognize that our understanding of the past changes as we uncover new evidence or ask different questions about the past and the traces left behind by people and institutions. As historian Faragher noted,

> Historical practice is very much determined by the things that people are concerned about. History is ultimately a moral art, and it is about values. It is not merely about the collection of facts. It is about the way we put those facts together and the meaning we give them. Arguments about facts are arguments about meaning. (as quoted in Stille, 2002)

Historians incorporate a variety of methods and address content that spans the globe. While the CCSS in history do not address specific content, we know that the study of history isn't possible without focusing on events in the past. When studying people in space and time, ELLs face specific content and linguistic challenges. For example, what content and linguistic challenges arise in the study of the long civil rights movement in the United States? As teachers, we need to consider what our students are equipped to do and what we need to be sure to emphasize. In the context of the long civil rights movement, can students, at a most basic content level, think chronologically and organize and understand the larger context of the history of race relations, housing, and labor in the United States? In the specific context of the larger concept, what does "long" refer to? What are civil rights? What makes something a movement? Students will need teachers' support with these concepts as they either learn about civil rights for the first time or challenge their prior understandings of civil rights.

The idea of a "long civil rights movement" instead of simply the civil rights movement brings to the fore the idea that history changes. How might students address changing narratives? Didn't the past simply happen, and can't we get the answer and move on? No! Students know that they don't always agree on "what happened" when they recount events in their daily lives. They must be taught that in order to explain their position carefully, they need to move beyond mere opinions and to instead support their claims with evidence. So it goes in the history classroom. In order to open the complexity of the past to students, teachers must problematize the past by posing challenging historical questions (Bain, 2005). And, teachers must help students develop the content and linguistic knowledge to make a claim and use evidence to support their arguments.

The purpose of using highly structured image analysis with ELLs is to establish their understanding of historians' heuristics (sourcing, contextualizing, and corroborating) and the importance of asking historical questions *before* they are asked to engage in these processes while simultaneously reading text that is often loaded with linguistic challenges. By using structured image analysis with ELLs, teachers can provide students with opportunities to practice engaging in historical thinking with high levels of initial support. ELLs can learn the language of the discipline, read images, and gain confidence in using the language before having to tackle reading text. As ELLs become more proficient in demonstrating these historical thinking competencies, teachers can gradually remove supports and then, ideally, engage ELLs in continued work with primary source images and with primary source documents.

## Pedagogical Practice: Picturing the Past to Build Historical Thinking Competencies

Teachers can use strategies in image analysis in order to build ELLs' linguistic competency in the context of historical thinking. The pedagogical practice outlined in this section has three points of focus: 1) building students' understanding of disciplinary concepts in history, 2) teaching them to apply discipline-specific language in source analysis, and 3) teaching students to assemble sources to support claims and make written arguments in order to prepare them to engage frequently with historical texts. The lesson outlined in this section works best as part of an introductory "What is History?" unit because it seeks to establish broad understandings about the language of the discipline and the ways historians think and work. The historical thinking competencies emphasized in this lesson will be discussed in the context of content that pertains to the long civil rights movement in U.S. history. Good historical inquiries start with a question, and for our purposes here, let's use the question: Why did African Americans need to fight for racial justice in the North?

Our traditional understanding of the civil rights movement often consists of the familiar ascension/declension narrative: The African American civil rights movement began in 1954 with the Supreme Court's *Brown v. Board of Education* decision, gathered steam through organized protests in the South, and emerged triumphant with the passing of the Civil Rights Act of 1964 and the Voting Rights Act of 1965. Decline followed these victories, precipitated by, among other things, the Vietnam War, black militancy, affirmative action, and bussing. Historians have noted shortcomings in this traditional narrative and have complicated our understanding of the actions of people in space and time by calling for the study of a "long civil rights movement." This long movement, rooted in activism beginning in the 1930s, stretches beyond the South and encompasses gender and class concerns in addition to the issues of race that remain at its core (Hall, 2005).

While students might be familiar with images of civil rights struggles in the South, images of the fight for racial equality in the North often receive little focus in textbooks; the limited photographs that do appear often emphasize urban riots. Image analysis can help students broaden their understanding of a long civil rights movement and help them use evidence to recognize and argue that the African American civil rights struggle was neither limited to the Southern section of the United States nor to the 1950s and 1960s.

Students operate in a visual culture, and given their access to digital technology, adolescents' fascination with themselves is easily and often recorded in images. Teachers might begin a lesson that emphasizes building historical literacy through image analysis by asking students to call up a selfie or another picture from their cell phones that recorded a specific, school-associated event. They should submit these images to the teacher digitally. If it is more appropriate, teachers can select pictures from their school website for this purpose. Regardless of how the images are obtained, the teacher should pose an open-ended (how or why) central historical question about the pictures as a whole. The question should invite discussion and evidence-based interpretation—not an opinion—and a successful response will need to state a claim and draw upon the images as evidence to support the claim. To draw students into historical inquiry, ask them to imagine that a historian—150 years in the future—has come across their pictures. This individual wants to answer the central historical question posed by the teacher. Now playing the role of a historian seeking to build a case based on primary sources, what questions should the students ask about the images? The purpose of this portion of the teaching strategy is to immerse ELLs in disciplinary literacy by teaching them how to "read" images while using the language of history.

When the process begins, it is important for teachers to first establish or review the definition of what constitutes a primary versus a secondary source. Using examples and nonexamples in the context of the specific image-based inquiry about a school event can help students distinguish between the two types of sources. In order to build ELLs' language skills and content knowledge simultaneously, as students begin to pose questions, direct them toward questions that emphasize analysis in context. Students might want to begin with a question like, "What is happening in each picture?" It might be difficult for students, who are steeped in the culture of their school and community, to realize that a person 150 years in the future will actually have no idea what is happening in the picture. Even if the picture "clearly" depicts an action, it is more appropriate to pose a question such as "What do you see?", because this type of question forces description and not inference (Seixas & Morton, 2013). Teachers should encourage students to avoid reading what they know into their questions and into possible responses to the questions. By encouraging students to treat their own images as "historical artifacts" that represent traces from "the past," teachers can begin to move ELLs toward an examination of sources as evidence.

As students pose questions they believe historians should ask about the images, teachers should record their ideas on the board and organize the questions into categories (to the extent possible) based on sourcing, contextualizing, and corroborating (see Table 1). Depending on the teachers' purposes, they can provide a definition of the three heuristics (sourcing, contextualizing, and corroborating) first and record students' contributions under each specific label, or they can record the students' questions in each category but only label the categories once students have exhausted their ideas. The latter approach can be beneficial if teachers pause and ask students to consider not just the questions they have asked but also the type of thinking involved in answering the questions and why they selected specific words in each question. For example, teachers might ask: what are all the questions labeled as sourcing questions asking you (students) to do? How does this type of thinking complement the questions that are aimed at contextualizing? What is different about the corroborating questions?

Teachers should use the language of history with students and help students recognize that in asking specific types of questions, they are using disciplinary concepts and engaging in these ways of thinking. In addition, while students might be tempted to trivialize the importance of questions in the context of history, teachers need to be sure to slow students down and to help them recognize that reciting the 5 Ws (who, what, where, when, why) can be a nice start, but in historical study, questions rarely have one-word answers. "Who" does literally mean who, and a specific name might work. But the name alone is not enough! In history, "who" demands that historians consider what this person's life was like, what the person might have been attempting to accomplish or

## Table 1. Examples of Student-Generated Sourcing (Group 1), Contextualizing (Group 2), and Corroborating (Group 3) Questions

| Group 1 | Group 2 | Group 3 |
|---------|---------|---------|
| Who wrote/created it?<br><br>When?<br><br>Who was the audience?<br>Who was supposed to see it?<br><br>Who was the author?<br><br>Famous? Not?<br><br>What else did he/she do? | What else was happening at the time?<br><br>How did people react?<br>Did they pay attention? Why/not?<br><br>Do people care about it now? Why/not?<br><br>Do people care about it now? Why/not?<br><br>What makes this time special or unique? | What did other people write?<br><br>What other pictures exist? Other artifacts?<br><br>What do books say about it? |

The teacher recorded and categorized students' questions, and then students were asked to note common features and label them using the language of history (sourcing, corroborating, contextualizing).

might have been advocating at that particular time, or what the worldview of the individual was. In order to assist ELLs in building their understanding of disciplinary concepts, they need numerous examples and opportunities to apply discipline-specific language in the process of source analysis. Teaching students to refer to questions as sourcing questions, contextualizing questions, and corroborating questions as they work with images will provide them with a mental structure upon which to hang ideas as they later encounter analysis of text-based primary sources.

Once teachers and students have organized their questions about images taken in their school, they should compare the questions they have developed as a class (based on the model in Table 1) to those in the PICS guide (Guide 1; Appendix A) provided in this chapter. What questions/ideas did they leave out? What questions/ideas did they include that were omitted in the PICS guide? It is important to be sure that students understand that in history we constantly reconsider and refine the questions we ask. If appropriate, students can then be asked to create captions for the pictures the teacher selected from the school event. Guide 2 (Appendix B) can serve as a basis to develop the captions. It is important for students to be sure to play the role of historians in the future when crafting the captions; again, they should not read their knowledge of the event into what is depicted in the image.

Once ELLs are comfortable with this initial introduction to the language of history, they can begin analyzing images using the content focus in this example, the long civil rights movement. In order to provide students with guidance and a purpose (and because the question asked often determines the extent to which a source can be used as evidence), teachers should pose the central historical question: Why did African Americans need to fight for racial justice in the North?

To begin considering the central historical question, but prior to digging into images, it might be useful for teachers to help students build background knowledge by examining maps of the civil rights movement. A variety of maps are available online, and teachers will quickly note the various stories that are told in the maps. Some maps document civil rights events in the South, some include Northern struggles, some focus on different years. By selecting two or three maps and using a similarities/differences model of comparison (focusing on the title of the map, the key, and specific information in the map), teachers can help students recognize that there cannot be one limited story of African Americans' fight for civil rights. Be sure to build students' competencies in the language of history by emphasizing that maps that were created after the time period being studied are secondary sources. To further draw attention to the nature of historical inquiry, invite students to pose questions about the maps. We want students to operate from the idea that history is about questions, not just answers.

After their attention is drawn to the idea that the struggle for civil rights was not limited to the South, provide students with various photos taken in Northern states prior to the mid-1950s (the traditional understanding of the start of the civil rights movement). The Organization of American Historians' (OAH's) *Magazine of History* (January 2012) devoted an issue, "Beyond Dixie" to the long civil rights movement, focusing on labor, open housing, poverty, the specific experiences of women, and desegregation in the North. This particular issue includes many images that teachers might deem appropriate for introducing students to or reinforcing their understanding of historical thinking concepts in the context of the long civil rights movement. Teachers might also find useful images in other issues from the OAH publication: "Martin Luther King, Jr." (January 2005); "Social Movements in the 1960s" (October 2006); and "Black Power" (July 2008). In addition to using this publication, teachers might locate images through the websites of the National Archives or Library of Congress. While various images can be appropriate given the context of the particular classroom, as an example, we'll use a photo taken in Chicago in 1941 outside of the Mid-City Realty Company. Because the purpose of this method is to teach students about the importance of sourcing, contextualizing, and corroborating sources as evidence, teachers should offer information about the photo in the form of a brief caption so that students can demonstrate their ability to engage in historical thinking competencies (Figure 3).

Using the PICS Analysis (Guide 1; Appendix A) in this chapter, lead students through an investigation of the image, keeping the central historical question in mind throughout the process. Help students recognize when they are engaging in sourcing, contextualizing, and corroborating questions as they work to note various aspects of the image. Repeat this process with several images so that students have multiple sources to consider. As students begin to improve their understanding of disciplinary methods in history and to apply the language of the discipline in source analysis, provide them with the opportunity to practice summarizing key content in context by having them write captions for the various images they have examined. Guide 2 (Appendix B) provides a model for this practice, and it includes a word bank consisting of words/phrases that are often used by historians to link ideas and consider evidence and perspective.

As teachers work with students to help them plan evidence-based arguments, Guide 3 (Appendix C) can provide structure. Remind students to address the teacher's central historical question and to use possible evidence from the images to help them articulate a claim. Guide 4 (Appendix D) then provides ELLs with a structured format that teachers can use to lead students in making a claim and using evidence from primary sources (while incorporating the language of history) to support this claim. Guide 5 (Appendix E) can be incorporated at any point in the process described above—either during source analysis or during writing an evidence-based argument—to help ELLs organize their specific examples/sources in the context of a larger historical concept.

The systematic method of image analysis outlined in this chapter is not unique; wise practitioners engage all students in detailed and discipline-specific source analysis in their classes on a daily basis. But it is especially important for teachers working with ELLs to consciously articulate the thinking processes that make up disciplinary literacy—even if very little reading of a text is involved. Building students' historical thinking competencies through image analysis has the potential to establish in ELLs a firm understanding of the central concepts and structure of the discipline of history. Once students have been steeped in the language of history, they can draw upon their established understandings of the discipline's content and linguistic challenges and be better prepared to meet textual complexity as they continue to work with primary and secondary sources.

## Reflection Questions and Action Plans

### Reflection Questions

1. What content is essential in the context of your teaching? How do the sources you select for your students have an impact on their understanding of the discipline? Why do you select the sources you select for use with your students? To what extent does the intellectual direction you set in your classes allow for students' linguistic development in the context of historical thinking?

2. Review a unit you have designed and/or taught previously. To what extent is your central historical question interpretive? How might you incorporate image analysis into this unit with the specific purpose of improving ELLs' disciplinary literacy? To what extent have you allowed opportunities for ELLs to "do" the discipline by questioning sources and crafting claims?

### Action Plans

Good history teaching often depends on questions. Practice writing open-ended (how/why) questions that problematize the past. Remember, history is about questions, not just answers!

Dimension 4 of the C3 Framework calls for students to take informed action based on conclusions they have drawn. How might you involve your students in consideration of the long civil rights movement in the context of their community? What potential sources might your students bring in that address contemporary concerns—triumphs or shortcomings—pertaining to the long civil rights movement? How might you help students convey their evidence-based conclusions in an appropriate public context?

## References

Achugar, M., & Schleppegrell, M. J. (2005). Beyond connectors: The construction of cause in history textbooks. *Linguistics and Education, 16,* 298–318.

Bain, R. B. (2005). "They thought the world was flat?": Applying the principles of how people learn in teaching high school history. In M. S. Donovan & J. D. Bransford (Eds.), *How students learn: History in the classroom* (pp. 179–213). Washington, DC: The National Academies Press.

Becker, C. L. (1932). Everyman his own historian. *American Historical Review, 37*(2), 221–236.

Britt, M. A., & Aglinskas, C. (2002). Improving students' ability to identify and use source information. *Cognition and Instruction, 20*(4), 485–522.

Bruner, J. S. (1960). *The process of education.* New York, NY: Vintage Books.

Coffin, C. (2006). *Historical discourse: The language of time, cause, and evaluation.* London, England: Continuum.

Collingwood, R. G. (1946/1994). *The idea of history* (revised ed.). Oxford, United Kingdom: Oxford University Press.

Danzer, G. A., & Newman, M. (1991). *Tuning in: Primary sources in the teaching of history.* Chicago, IL: The World History Project.

de Oliveira, L. C. (2011). *Knowing and writing school history: The language of students' expository writing and teachers' expectations.* Charlotte, NC: Information Age Publishing.

Drake, F. D., & Nelson, L. R. (2009). *Engagement in teaching history: Theory and practices for middle and secondary teachers* (2nd ed.). Upper Saddle River, NJ: Pearson Education.

Fang, Z., & Coatoam, S. (2013). Disciplinary literacy: What you want to know about it. *Journal of Adolescent & Adult Literacy, 55*(8), 627–632.

Fang, Z., & Schleppegrell, M. J. (2008). *Reading in secondary content areas: A language-based pedagogy.* Ann Arbor, MI: University of Michigan Press.

Fang, Z., Sun, Y., Chiu, C., & Trutschel, B. (2014). Inservice teachers' perception of a language-based approach to content area reading. *Australian Journal of Language and Literacy, 37*(1), 55–66.

Gabella, M. S. (1994). Beyond the looking glass: Bringing students into the conversation of historical inquiry. *Theory and Research in Social Education, 22*(3), 340–363.

Hall, J. D. (2005). The long civil rights movement and the political uses of the past. *Journal of American History, 91*(4), 1233–1263.

Halliday, M. A. K., & Matthiessen, C. M. (2004). *An introduction to functional grammar.* London, England: Arnold.

Lee, P. (2005). Putting principles into practice: Understanding history. In M. S. Donovan & J. D. Bransford (Eds.), *How students learn: History in the classroom* (pp. 31–77). Washington, DC: The National Academies Press.

Levstik, L. (2000). Articulating the silences: Teachers' and adolescents' conceptions of historical significance. In P. Stearns, P. Seixas, & S. Wineburg (Eds.), *Knowing, teaching, and learning history: National and international perspectives* (pp. 284–305). New York, NY: New York University Press.

Moje, E. B. (2008). Foregrounding the disciplines in secondary literacy teaching and learning: A call for change. *Journal of Adolescent & Adult Literacy, 52*(2), 96–107.

Monte-Sano, C. (2008). Qualities of historical writing instruction: A comparative case study of two teachers' practices. *American Educational Research Journal, 45*(4), 1045–1079.

Monte-Sano, C. (2011a). Beyond reading comprehension and summary: Learning to read and write in history by focusing on evidence, perspective, and interpretation. *Curriculum Inquiry, 41*(2), 212–249.

Monte-Sano, C. (2011b). Learning to open up history for students: Preservice teachers' emerging pedagogical content knowledge. *Journal of Teacher Education, 62*(3), 260–272.

Monte-Sano, C., & Cochran, M. (2009). Attention to learners, subject, or teaching: What takes precedence as preservice candidates learn to teach historical thinking and reading? *Theory and Research in Social Education, 37*(1), 101–135.

Monte-Sano, C., De La Paz, S., & Felton, M. (2014a). Implementing a disciplinary-literacy curriculum for US history: Learning from expert middle school teachers in diverse classrooms. *Journal of Curriculum Studies, 46*(4), 540–575.

Monte-Sano, C., De La Paz, S., & Felton, M. (2014b). *Reading, thinking, and writing history: Teaching argument writing to diverse learners in the Common Core classroom, grades 6-12.* New York, NY: Teachers College Press.

National Council for the Social Studies. (2013). *The college, career, and civic life (C3) framework for social studies state standards: Guidance for enhancing the rigor of K–12 civics, economics, geography, and history.* Silver Spring, MD: Author.

National Governors Association Center for Best Practices & Council of Chief State School Officers. (2010). *Common Core State Standards for English language arts & literacy in history/social studies, science, and technical subjects.* Washington, DC: Authors. Retrieved from: http://www.corestandards.org/ELA-Literacy/

Nokes, J. D. (2011). Recognizing and addressing the barriers to adolescents' "reading like historians." *The History Teacher, 44*(3), 379–404.

Nokes, J. D., Dole, J. A., & Hacker, D. J. (2007). Teaching high school students to use heuristics while reading historical texts. *Journal of Educational Psychology, 99*(3), 492–504.

Organization of American Historians. (2005). Martin Luther King, Jr. *Magazine of History, 19*(1).

Organization of American Historians. (2006). Social movements in the 1960s. *Magazine of History, 20*(5).

Organization of American Historians. (2008). Black power. *Magazine of History, 22*(3).

Organization of American Historians. (2012). Beyond Dixie: The Black freedom struggle outside of the south. *Magazine of History, 26*(1).

Reisman, A. (2012a). Reading like a historian: A document-based history curriculum intervention in urban high schools. *Cognition and Instruction, 30*(1), 86–112.

Reisman, A. (2012b). The "document-based lesson": Bringing disciplinary inquiry into high school history classrooms with adolescent struggling readers. *Journal of Curriculum Studies, 44*(2), 233–264.

Schleppegrell, M. J., Achugar, M., & Oteiza, T. (2004). The grammar of history: Enhancing content-based instruction through a functional focus on language. *TESOL Quarterly, 38*, 67–93.

Schleppegrell, M. J., & de Oliveira, L. C. (2006). An integrated language and content approach for history teachers. *Journal of English for Academic Purposes, 5*, 254–268.

Schleppegrell, M. J., Greer, S., & Taylor, S. (2008). Literacy in history: Language and meaning. *Australian Journal of Language and Literacy, 31*(2), 174–187.

Schleppegrell, M. J., & O'Hallaron, C. L. (2011). Teaching academic language in L2 secondary settings. *Annual Review of Applied Linguistics, 31*, 3–18.

Schlissel, L. (1982/1992). *Women's diaries of the westward journey.* New York, NY: Schocken Books.

Seixas, P. (1998). Student teachers thinking historically. *Theory and Research in Social Education, 26*(3), 310–341.

Seixas, P. (1999). Beyond "content" and "pedagogy": In search of a way to talk about history education. *Journal of Curriculum Studies, 31*(3), 317–337.

Seixas, P., & Morton, T. (2013). *The big six historical thinking concepts.* Toronto, ON: Nelson Education.

Shanahan, T., & Shanahan, C. (2008). Teaching disciplinary literacy to adolescents: rethinking content-area literacy. *Harvard Educational Review, 78*(1), 40–59.

Stille, A. (2002, June 29). Textbook publishers learn to avoid messing with Texas. *New York Times.* Retrieved from http://www.nytimes.com/2002/06/29/arts/29TEXT.html?emc=eta1

Sugrue, T. J. (2008). *Sweet land of liberty: The forgotten struggle for civil rights in the North.* New York, NY: Random House.

Suh, Y., & Grant, L. W. (2014). Assessing ways of seeing the past: Analysis of the use of historical images and student performance in the NAEP US history assessment. *The History Teacher, 48*(1), 71–90.

Vachon, J. (Photographer). (1941). Picket line in front of Mid-City Realty Company, South Chicago, Illinois [Photograph]. Library of Congress. Retrieved from http://www.loc.gov/pictures/item/fsa2000043792/PP/

Wineburg, S. (2001). *Historical thinking and other unnatural acts: Charting the future of teaching the past.* Philadelphia, PA: Temple University Press.

Wineburg, S., Martin, D., & Monte-Sano, C. (2011). *Reading like a historian: Teaching literacy in middle and high school history classrooms.* New York, NY: Teachers College Press.

# Appendix A: Guide 1. PICS Analysis

## A Guide to Using Photographs as Possible Evidence

Historical Question Being Investigated:

**P**:   Place—Where was the picture taken? How do you know? What clues help you decide?

_____

_____

**I**:   In Time—Was the picture taken long ago or in recent times? How can you tell? Is a date given?

_____

_____

**C**:   Context—What was happening at this place during this time? What people or events might make this time or place important?

Context of Time Period: _____

_____

Context of Place: _____

_____

**S**:   See—What can you see in the picture? Divide the picture into two or four parts. What do you notice in each part?

| Part 1. People? Words? Objects? | Part 2. People? Words? Objects? |
|---|---|
| Part 3. People? Words? Objects? | Part 4. People? Words? Objects? |

## PICS Analysis: A Guide to Using Photographs as Possible Evidence

Who took this picture? _____

How might that person want you to feel when you look at it? What details in the photo make you feel that way? What might have been the photographer's purpose?

_____

_____

Write a question you would ask the photographer. _____

_____

**Pictures in Context:** How might you use the details in the picture to understand what is happening to people at this time and in this place?

| Part 1. Details in Context: | Part 2. Details in Context: |
|---|---|
| | |
| Part 3. Details in Context: | Part 4. Details in Context: |
| | |

What questions do you have about the picture *as a source*? What other information would you like to know?

_____

_____

# Appendix B: Guide 2. Writing Captions to Weave Context

Captions are brief explanations that usually accompany a picture or an illustration. They provide information about the image.

Write a caption for each image. In your caption, include what you think is the most important information from the *PICS Guide* that will help people who are not familiar with the picture understand it.

Picture #  _____

**P:** _____

**I:** _____

**C:** _____

**S:** Instead of telling the viewer what *you see*, *write a question* for a person who is looking at the picture. Use "how" or "why" to begin your question.

_____

_____

Use the information above to write your caption for the picture. Write two or three sentences. Remember to place the picture in its historical context, focusing on **people** in **space** and **time**. You might use some of the words in the box below in your caption.

| while | which is supported by | gave rise to |
| suggests | in effect | in addition |
| for example | for this reason | was caused by |

_____

_____

_____

_____

_____

_____

# Appendix C: Guide 3. Planning an Argument With Evidence From Photographs

**Pictures as Possible Evidence:** How might you use the details in each picture as evidence to answer the historical question you are investigating and make a claim? Read the question again, and look at the details you wrote down on the PICS Guide. Where do the sources agree? Where do they disagree?

PIC # _____ as Possible Evidence:

PIC # _____ as Possible Evidence:

PIC # _____ as Possible Evidence:

PIC # _____ as Possible Evidence:

**Thesis/Claim:** _____

_____

_____

_____

_____

_____

# Appendix D: Guide 4. Making an Argument With Evidence From Photographs

Historical Question Being Investigated:

Thesis/Claim: _____

_____

_____

*To organize support for your thesis/claim, use the following guide for each picture.*

This primary source can be used to support my argument because the picture, taken on

_____ in _____
            (date)                         (location)

shows _____
                       (what you see in the picture)

_____

The details in the picture suggest that African Americans were treated unfairly in

_____ because _____
            (location)                    (describe what was unfair)

_____

The picture supports my thesis because _____
                               (supporting evidence in context)

_____. I wonder

_____

(note any questions you have about the source or how it relates to other sources)

# Appendix E: Guide 5. Historical Evidence: The Long Civil Rights Movement

|  | **LONG** | **CIVIL RIGHTS** | **MOVEMENT** |
|---|---|---|---|
|  | Time:<br><br>Duration, over several years.<br><br>When and where did the action take place? | Things:<br><br>Power or privileges to which citizens are entitled.<br><br>What rights did people seek? | Actions:<br><br>Series of organized activities working toward an end.<br><br>How were people taking organized action? |
| PIC # |  |  |  |
| PIC # |  |  |  |
| PIC # |  |  |  |
| PIC # |  |  |  |

**How might the civil rights sought and the actions taken serve as evidence to help you answer the central historical question?**

_____

_____

_____

_____

_____

_____

_____

_____

# The Past Is Only Slightly Less Murky Than the Future: Corroborating Multiple Sources From Art and History

*Rhoda Coleman, University of Southern California*

*Jeff Zwiers, Stanford University*

The most powerful way to develop language is through lots of authentic communication. This means reading, writing, listening, speaking, and conversing about interesting things to get something meaningful done. Yet in recent decades, we have veered off course onto one that has been weighed down by excessive teaching about language, meaning the teaching of disconnected vocabulary and grammar rules, rather than rich modeling and teaching of ways to use language in disciplinary ways. Many students, particularly ELLs, have been severely "underimmersed" in authentic communication experiences across disciplines.

In most secondary settings, the bulk of the day is focused on content with a small portion focused on language, if that. These settings fail to leverage the potential of content lessons, with their many rich ideas and activities, to develop language. One of the most important uses of language is to communicate how we interpret the world, its events, and the various perspectives of past and present people in it.

In this chapter, we focus on developing language and thinking in history lessons with a procedure that capitalizes on the use of visual arts. The procedure provides students with a rigorous, yet scaffolded, approximation of what historians do as they analyze, interpret, and discuss different sources and perspectives around a historical event. The procedure emphasizes original interpretation of art and other sources, as well as authentic communication between students. We place special emphasis on the activities and scaffolding that build language and serve the needs of ELLs.

Art is a motivator, engaging in itself. Besides being visually stimulating, it evokes a variety of emotions to connect students to content they might not ordinarily find interesting. Crespin (1998) provides such descriptors as calm, distressing, war-like, aggressive, harmonious, joyous, tranquil, turbulent, threatening, lively, dull, active, serious.

In the following sections, we explain the linguistic challenges that historical thinking and communicating can pose for ELLs, and then we share a procedure for teachers to use to better meet the linguistic demands for ELLs in engaging in rigorous, grade-level disciplinary thinking and communicating.

## The Common Core State Standards and Specific Demands for ELLs

### Content Demands

The new Common Core State Standards (CCSS) for English Language Arts & Literacy in History/ Social Studies, Science, and Technical Subjects (National Governors Association Center for Best Practices [NGA] & Council of Chief State School Officers [CCSSO], 2010) provide us with the best of many worlds. As teachers and teacher educators who have witnessed the theoretical pendulum swing so many times, we welcome the opportunity to have a curriculum that gives balanced attention to both literary and informational text; to both foundational skills and to critical thinking integrated across the curriculum; and to clear, rigorous standards that still allow for teacher creativity, expertise, and professionalism in making instructional choices to achieve these standards.

The lesson presented here integrates the CCSS English language arts (ELA) standards with California State Board of Education history/social science content standards (1998) and visual (and performing) arts standards (2001), with strategies to make content accessible for ELLs (Table 1).

In social studies, we have only listed those pertaining to a 6th-grade lesson as an example of a lesson featured here. However, the possibilities are limited only by the teacher's access to works of art related to the particular historic content being taught. Regardless of the content area, here are historical thinking skills to consider:

1. **Taking multiple perspectives.** Taking multiple perspectives can be difficult for ELLs because this skill tends to depend on their exposure to a wide range of texts and videos that show other perspectives, as well as previous schooling experiences that may not have emphasized this type of thinking when learning history.

2. **Using primary and secondary sources and inferring biases in them.** Many ELLs have not been challenged to consider where information in history books comes from. They have not been asked to be critical readers and question the truth and motivations of authors of texts (Rozenzweig & Wineburg, n.d.).

3. **Comparing and contrasting interpretations using multiple primary sources** (Schrum, n.d.). Many ELLs have not had practice reading primary sources, which are not written for students, much less language learners. Comparing and contrasting requires them to pick out key similarities and differences of the texts, which they might not have done before.

## Table 1. Selected Standards

| THE STANDARDS |
| --- |

| **COMMON CORE STATE STANDARDS FOR ENGLISH LANGUAGE ARTS & LITERACY IN HISTORY/SOCIAL STUDIES, SCIENCE, AND TECHNICAL SUBJECTS**<br>(National Governors Association for Best Practices & Council of Chief State School Officers, 2010) |
| --- |

**Reading Standards for Informational Text 6–12 (p. 39)**

RI.6.1. Cite textual evidence to support analysis of what the text says explicitly [emphasis added] as well as inferences [emphasis added] drawn from the text.

RI.6.6. Determine an author's point of view or purpose in a text and explain how it is conveyed in the text.

RI.6.7. Integrate information presented in different media or formats (e.g. visually, quantitatively) as well as in words to develop a coherent understanding of a topic or issue.

RI.6.9. Compare and contrast one author's presentation of events with that of another (e.g. a memoir written by and a biography written of the same person.)

RI.7.9. Analyze how two or more authors writing about the same topic shape their presentations of key information by emphasizing different evidence or advancing different interpretations of facts.

RI.8.9. Analyze a case in which two or more texts provide conflicting information on the same topic and identify where the texts disagree on matters of fact or interpretation.

**Writing Standards 6–12 (p. 42)**

W.6.1. Write arguments to support claims with clear reasons and relevant evidence.
- a. Introduce claim(s) and organize the reasons and evidence clearly.
- b. Support claim(s) with clear reasons and relevant evidence, using credible sources and demonstrating an understanding of the topic or text.
- c. Use words, phrases, and clauses to clarify the relationships among claim(s) and reasons.
- d. Establish and maintain a formal style.
- e. Provide a concluding statement or section that follows from the argument presented

**College and Career Readiness Anchor Standards for Speaking and Listening (p. 48)**

*Comprehension and Collaboration*
1. Prepare for and participate effectively in a range of conversations and collaborations with diverse partners, building on others' ideas and expressing their own clearly and persuasively.
2. Integrate and evaluate information presented in diverse media and formats, including visually, quantitatively, and orally.
3. Evaluate a speaker's point of view, reasoning, and use of evidence and rhetoric.

| **VISUAL AND PERFORMING ARTS CONTENT STANDARDS: GRADE 6**<br>California Department of Education (2001) |
| --- |

**1.0. Artistic Perception**

*Develop Perceptual Skills and Visual Arts Vocabulary*
- 1.1. Identify and describe all the elements of art found in selected works of art (e.g., color, shape/form, line, texture, space, value).
- 1.2. Discuss works of art as to theme, genre, style, idea, and differences in media.
- 1.3. Describe how artists can show the same theme by using different media and styles.

**4.0. Aesthetic Valuing**

*Derive Meaning*
- 4.1. Construct and describe plausible interpretations of what they perceive in works of art.
- 4.2. Identify and describe ways in which their culture is being reflected in current works of art.

| **HISTORY–SOCIAL SCIENCE CONTENT STANDARDS**<br>California Department of Education (1998) |
| --- |

6.7. Students analyze the geographic, political, economic, religious, and social structures during the development of Rome.
1. Identify the location and describe the rise of the Roman Republic, including the importance of such . . . historical figures as . . . Julius Caesar . . .
3. Identify the location of and the political and geographic reasons for the growth of Roman territories and expansion of the empire . . .
4. Discuss the influence of Julius Caesar . . . in Rome's transition from republic to empire.

The History–Social Science Content Standards (California Department of Education, 1998) are the example from the sample lesson.

4. **Arguing and supporting claims with evidence** (Schrum, n.d.). Many ELLs have not had school experiences that have given them practice in making their own claims and then supporting them. They have not had experience figuring what counts as evidence and how strong or weak it is, according to the expectations in a given discipline.

5. **Understanding context by making connections between events chronologically and geographically.** Many ELLs have thought of history as the memorization of what happened, what people did, and when. They have not had much practice being detectives and making connections on their own. The notion of going outside the textbook and generating new ideas is very different from what they expect to do in history class.

These may seem like a lot of standards for one series of lessons, but we will present a systematic and accessible way to integrate all of these across these three content areas with English language development (ELD) strategies.

## Linguistic Demands

Integrating the visual arts with ELA and history/social science provides one obvious tool to make content comprehensible to ELLs, that of visual clues. However, looking at the ELD standards from California (California State Board of Education, 2012), we can see that integrating across content areas also provides opportunities for meeting the linguistic demands of ELLs (and all learners) in multiple ways. Receptive and expressive academic language demands include using:

- **argument language**, which consists of the language for making a claim, supporting it with evidence, and explaining how the evidence supports the claim (NGA & CCSSO, 2010).

- **compare and contrast language** for analyzing multiple accounts of the same event and multiple sources.

- **descriptive language** to analyze an image.

- **expanded and enriched language** as students describe a painting and its features.

- **strategies and conventions for writing cohesively** when writing arguments and conclusions.

- **strategies for reading the language of complex sentences** to determine key ideas from historical sources.

We will explore these demands in greater depth as we describe the pedagogical practice. We will look at several pieces of artwork relevant to sixth-grade and eighth-grade curricula, keeping in mind that artwork pertaining to any grade level may be used. We will suggest several other paintings that can be used with other topics.

After analyzing the work for artistic elements and details, we will analyze it for the message it is conveying about the content. Students will then compare the artist's account to other primary and secondary sources of the same event and draw conclusions by comparing and contrasting points of view.

# Rationale

Argumentation is a vital skill across disciplines, though it takes on different forms and flavors as students switch classes. In order to generate and support an argument in history, a person needs to first be able to analyze and interpret evidence in and from various sources. This "building historical thinking skills" approach to history teaching is very different from the common emphasis on teaching students to memorize events and dates. This approach focuses on *using* knowledge of the past to construct new insights and questions (Wineburg, 2001).

The interpretation of art gives students practice in putting images into words as they describe a painting to one another. Students can "enter into a dialogue that can provide access to the meaning of the work of art" (Crespin, 1998, p. i–ii). This provides ELLs of different proficiency levels multiple possible levels of access to participating. Analyzing images also offers the chance to develop skills of interpreting art, particularly the skill of inferring the artist's purpose(s) for using various techniques, colors, and subjects. This will help students as they encounter and interpret a wide range of images and artwork in the future, including the images used to describe current events in the news. Finally, the use of art as a source of evidence in historical inquiry teaches students to use a wide range of artifacts in the building of ideas and arguments in history (Suh, 2013). Art introduces us to the historical and cultural context of the artwork. Stokstad (2005) describes how artists throughout time have used art to promote political and educational agendas. Therefore, we can explore whether the artwork is consciously enlisted to serve social ends or to please a patron, or is purely for self-expression.

Visual support is provided not only by examining works of art, but also through the use of graphic organizers to see relationships, make connections, and organize ideas when interpreting through reading and listening. Visual supports for thinking and language, as Hill and Miller (2013) explain, are very important for ELLs because they need extra support in visualizing the events and connections between them. Along with sentence starters and sentence frames, graphic organizers support structuring these events and connections for production of language when writing and speaking.

The large amount of oral work in this activity attempts to address a grave need in many schools with significant numbers of diverse learners: students learning to clearly articulate and support academic ideas (Soto-Hinman, 2011). ELLs need ample opportunities for authentic and functional English use to acquire high levels of proficiency. They need tasks focusing on productive verbal exchanges that are structured to prepare them for successful interactions with both other ELLS and with proficient English speakers (Goldenberg & Coleman, 2010). Without scaffolding and practice, this vital life skill does not develop. Indeed, many underperforming schools, desperate to raise test scores, have developed ingrained pedagogical habits that do not include appropriate attention to building students' oral abilities. The following pedagogical practice attempts to model ways in which teachers can develop oral language both for and through content learning in order to meet multiple new standards.

## Pedagogical Practice: Corroborating Multiple Sources From Art and History for ELLs

The pedagogical practice begins with a teacher-guided analysis and interpretation of primary and secondary sources. During modeling and discussion in this stage, the teacher models for students the thinking and language used by historians who engage in a process like this one. The teacher also offers time for students to practice thinking and using this language in brief pair-shares interspersed throughout the discussions. This frequent practice in speaking and listening to peers' thoughts builds language and refines thinking. This pedagogical practice supports students to think historically in the interpretation of one or more works of art.

This pedagogical practice contains four parts that work together to support the learning of the standards described above:

1. Analysis

2. Oral Language Development

3. Conclusion

4. Assessment

Following is a description of each of the four sections, accompanied by a description of a sample lesson.

## 1. Analysis

Analysis of content through primary and secondary sources. Students:

a. Discuss the reliability of primary and secondary sources and why we need to look at more than one source.

b. Look at art for getting into the text and for artistic features.

c. Read the text.

d. Revisit the art to compare/contrast and add new insights to what they see/don't see in the art.

e. Analyze the primary source.

f. Revisit the art to compare/contrast the primary source to the art.

As an illustration of this practice, we use a painting, "Vercingetorix Throws Down Arms at the Feet of Julius Caesar" (Figure 1; Royer, 1899).

The first step is to analyze the artwork. This illustration is found in a sixth-grade textbook (Burstein & Shek, 2006, p. 353). Upon presenting this image to the students, point out the date, 1899. Initiate a class discussion with questions and guidance such as:

• What is the difference between a primary and secondary source? (Explain the purpose of analyzing and comparing these primary and secondary sources. E.g., to understand the different perspectives of different people involved.) Are the sources reliable?

*Figure 1. Vercingetorix Throws Down Arms at the Feet of Julius Caesar (Royer, 1899)*

- I'm not sure what this is supposed to be representing or if it really happened like that. How can I find out if it is an accurate portrayal since Royer wasn't an eyewitness?

- What do you see happening in this painting? What are some details you see?

- Who does Royer make the focus of the painting? What techniques does he use to show the focus?

- Who are the other figures you see in this painting? What are they doing?

- Who has the power, the heroic qualities? Why do you think so? Who has the least power?

- What techniques does the artist use to communicate feelings of nobility, bravery, stoicism, humility, or dignity?

- What is the artist's purpose in painting this scene?

- The text doesn't tell me much about the painting. Why does this event matter? Is it historically significant? How can I find out?

After this discussion, ask students to look at the artwork with a partner and describe to one another what they see in detail. You can encourage the use of certain art terms such as *symmetry, contrast, mood, composition*. The teacher may find other avenues for discussion using the art analysis questions (Table 2).

As the students continue to work with a partner or individually, they record information on the "Analyzing an Image" graphic organizer (Figure 2).

## Table 2. Art Analysis Questions

**Art Analysis Questions**

**BEFORE comparing the artwork to other sources**
*Content*
- When and where was the work created? What is its date and title?
- Who created the work and what is the point of view? How do you know?
- Who was the intended audience?
- What is the content of the painting, whom do you see, where is this happening, what is happening, what is included?
- Who is the focus? How does the artist let you know the focus?
- What is the patronage? What does the patronage tell you about the point of view?
- What seem to be the attitudes of the characters?
- What was valued?
- What are some details that tell you about the time and culture?
- What emotions does it evoke? Why?
- What do you think was the artist's purpose in painting it?
- What questions do you have about the artwork? (Record questions)

*Artistic elements*
- How does the artist communicate through such techniques as line, color, brushwork, tactile values, modeling, proportion, perspective or special construction, and composition?
- Is there a style of the period or the culture?

**AFTER comparing to the other sources:**
- What decisive moment was chosen?
- What is left out?
- Whose point of view is absent?
- What is present that is not supported by the text or is contradicted by the text?
- Is anything included symbolic rather than literal?
- Is the artist making a personal or political statement?
- What questions does the artwork raise about society and culture?

Adapted with permission from Hutton (2014), Kleinfelder (1998), Siegenthaler (1999), and Stokstad (2005).

A key document in this lesson is the graphic organizer "Comparing Multiple Sources" (Figure 3). Record students' observations, questions, and conclusions about the art on the graphic organizer under Artist's Version. The questions and sources used on this graphic organizer can be adjusted to suit the resources found. More than one piece of art may be examined.

The next step is to read the textbook. This is read after the painting analysis so that students do not bring too much prior knowledge to their initial analysis. Students read about the topic as presented in the textbook, or perhaps in an article (secondary source). The text caption in this example states, "Julius Caesar conquered Gaul and added it to his empire. This painting from the late 1800s shows a Frankish leader surrendering to Caesar by dropping his weapons at Caesar's feet" (Burstein & Shek, 2006, pp. 353).

In this text, there is little said about Vercingetorix, not even his name. However, there is a lot of information about Julius Caesar, the other major figure in the painting. The textbook goes on to discuss Caesar's rise to power, the Gallic Wars, his conflicts with Pompey and the Roman Senate, and his death. Discussion questions might be, "What does the textbook say about Julius Caesar and

## Analyzing an Image

**Image:**

|  | Sample Prompts | Observations | Possible Inferences |
|---|---|---|---|
| **WHO** is in the image? | What role or occupations? What status (rich or poor)? If several people, are they related to each other? |  |  |
| **WHAT** are the people doing? | What actions? What objects are used? What is the focus of attention? |  |  |
| **WHERE** does the image take place? | In what region or country? In what setting? What is the terrain? Are there landmarks? |  |  |
| **WHEN** did the action in the image take place? | What time of day? What time of year? What historical period? |  |  |
| **WHY** is the action happening? | What reasons might there be for the actions? Does the background suggest a purpose? What might happen next? |  |  |

Summary explanation:

*Figure 2. Analyzing an Image*

Adapted with permission from Hutton, L. (2014). *The history project*. Long Beach, CA: California State University, Long Beach & Dominguez Hills.

the Gallic Wars? Whose voice is not heard in the textbook account? Why is this painting included in the textbook? Why do you think the Frankish leader is not named? Who is he?" At this point, return to the graphic organizer "Comparing Multiple Sources" (Figure 3) and enter information in the Textbook column.

It is now time to bring in a firsthand account, or primary source. Using whole class discussion and pair-shares, coanalyze excerpts of the primary source *Caesar's Gallic War* while referring to the "Analyzing a Document" questions (Table 3). Add these conclusions to the "Comparing Multiple Sources" graphic organizer (Figure 3). Questions might include:

- Who wrote this document?

- Where and when was it written?

**Comparing Multiple Sources**

Title:

| | Artist's Version<br>Title/Artist: | Textbook Version | Primary Source #1<br>Title/Author: | Primary Source #2<br>Title/Author: |
|---|---|---|---|---|
| What type of work is it?<br>What year was it produced?<br>When? By whom? | | | | |
| What is the focus of the content? | | | | |
| What is the point of view?<br>How do you know? | | | | |
| Whose point of view is absent? | | | | |
| What new details or information does it introduce? | | | | |
| How does it connect to the bigger picture? | | | | |

*Figure 3. Comparing Multiple Sources*

## Table 3. Analyzing a Document

### Analyzing a Document

**Type of Document**
- What type of document is it?
- How does this information help you understand this document?

**Author**
- Who wrote the document?
- What is the author's occupation, background, etc.?
- How does this information help you understand this document?

**Audience**
- Who was the document written for?
- How does this information help you understand this document?

**Context**
- Where was this written?
- When was this written?
- What important things were going on at the time that relate to the document?
- How does this information help you understand this document?

**Content**
- What is the author saying?
- What details are important?
- What is the main idea of the document?

**Purpose**
- Why is the author writing this document?
- Does the author want something specific to happen by writing this document?

Adapted with permission from Hutton, L. (2014). *The history project*. Long Beach, CA: California State University, Long Beach & Dominguez Hills.

- According to Caesar's account of the Gallic Wars, what is his version of the events depicted in this painting? (Notice it is written in the third person although written by Caesar about himself.)

- What is the main idea?

- What was his purpose for writing this?

- What new information did you find out? Do we know if it is accurate?

- Whose point of view is absent?

Students may also work in pairs to record on the "Evidence Collection" graphic organizer (Figure 4).

Have students write a brief paragraph supporting the point of view of one of the resources. An adaptation of the "Drawing Conclusions" framework (Figure 5) may be used as a support. Students may use the graphic organizer recording form and also find additional sources to find out why Vercingetorix is considered a hero in France or to read Plutarch's account. For example, why

**Evidence Collection: Observing and Questioning a Source**

**Source:**_____

Is this a primary or secondary source?_____

How do you know? _____

_____

What observations can you make about this source?

| | |
|---|---|
| Type of Document | Author |
| Audience | Context |
| Content | Purpose |

Adapted with permission from Hutton, L. (2014). *The history project*. Long Beach, CA: California State University, Long Beach & Dominguez Hills.

After looking at this source, what can you conclude about (topic)?

_____

_____

_____

_____

_____

_____

*Figure 4. Evidence Collection*

did Napoleon III commission Frédéric Bartholdi to sculpt *The Statue of Vercingetorix*, in Clermont-Ferrand, France? Interpreting an artwork means not only understanding the context of the subject's time, but also the context and political motivations of the time the artwork was created, which may be many hundreds or thousands of years after the event depicted. This is certainly true of Vercingetorix (Haywood, 2009; Beardsley, 2013).

To consolidate the learning of the analysis portion of the lesson, students may use the "Drawing Conclusions" graphic organizer (Figure 5).

**Drawing Conclusions**

**Focus Question:**

Use the information collected from a primary or secondary source to draw conclusions about _____
_____.

Cite examples from the source to support your conclusion.

Write your response in a paragraph.

---

Helpful Hints:

    Topic sentence: State the answer to the question.

    Supporting details: Cited from sources

    Sample sentence starters:

- According to _____
- As stated in _____
- Based on the information in _____
- Based on the details from _____
- The details from _____ suggest _____
- From _____ (diary, quote, account) you can tell that
  _____

- From this _____, you can conclude that _____

_____

_____

_____

_____

_____

_____

_____

*Figure 5. Drawing Conclusions*

Adapted with permission from Hutton, L. (2014). *The history project*. Long Beach, CA: California State University, Long Beach & Dominguez Hills.

## 2. Oral Language

Oral language development is of two kinds: collaborative group work and paired conversations.

### Collaborative Group Work

In the group work stage of the pedagogical practice, students in a group (of four or more) take on the perspective of an artist who depicted the event, an author who wrote about the event, or a participant in the event. This allows students to synthesize the ideas generated in the previous analysis stage and do something interesting with them. Students work together to form an oral paragraph, which encourages them to develop their abilities to form responses beyond the one-word and one-sentence levels. They practice three times with three different partners within their group to make their responses stronger and clearer each time (Zwiers, O'Hara, & Pritchard, 2014). They borrow ideas and language from previous partners to form the strongest (in terms of evidence) and clearest (in terms of language) response possible. This activity allows students to start with an oral "rough draft" and build up their ideas through scaffolded interactions with others.

Then, students share their perspective paragraphs with members of other groups in the same successive partner format. This allows them to learn other perspectives and further refine their own responses. The teacher formatively assesses the interactions and then has several students, each from one of the perspectives, share their ideas with the whole class; this sets up the next activity, which is focused on conversations.

For this lesson, the teacher divides the class into two groups to take on the perspectives of either Vercingetorix/Royer or Julius Caesar using the brief conclusion paragraphs they created.

The teacher models how to write a monologue using a perspective that wasn't present, in this example Plutarch. The teacher covers the notes and orally shares a version of the monologue without memorizing it. Each group then discusses ideas to generate a "perspective monologue" for their person's perspective. Students in each group then discuss what their person would say if asked for his perspective on the event: "My name is _____ and here is my perspective on the Gallic Wars and its importance."

Students practice their perspective monologues orally in pairs with two different members who are using the same perspective to refine ideas each time. This allows each student to become expert on his or her assigned person by sharing ideas about the same person with others in his or her group. For example, within the Julius Caesar group, partners take turns practicing with one another what Caesar would say about the event. They may borrow ideas from one another to improve their own monologues on Caesar. The two partners then share their improved monologues with another partner team, who are also taking on Caesar's perspective.

Students dissolve their groups and meet with members of other groups, in pairs, to share their perspective monologues. A student from the Royer group shares her perspective monologue with a member of the Julius Caesar group. The teacher encourages them to improve their monologues each time they share.

Optionally, have students write down their final perspective monologue before sharing it, instead of memorizing it.

## Paired Conversations

Students then engage in the back-and-forth building of ideas through paired constructive conversations (Zwiers, O'Hara, & Pritchard, 2014). Students have been learning to use several key conversation skills to build and choose academic ideas with others during lessons. These skills include clarifying, supporting ideas with evidence, and evaluating and choosing sides when there are two or more perspectives, as is the case here. Students are asked to decide which perspective is the most important to be included in an account of the event being studied. This forces them to consider the various perspectives that they formed and learned through analysis of sources and listening to their classmates. They do not have to argue for the perspective that they assumed in the previous activity, but the final decision must be well reasoned, and all students need to be able to articulate it to you.

Have students from two different perspectives meet in pairs and put on their historian hats to argue the prompt: If a new history book only has room for one perspective of this event, which one should it include? How could the textbook give a more balanced view?

A student from the Julius Caesar group meets with a student who was in the Royer group. They can argue whether Caesar's or Royer's perspective should be presented in the book.

The teacher observes students to assist them in working on clarifying, supporting, and evaluating ideas during their conversations. Students may refer back to their various recording forms. The teacher observes the students and prompts them to ask questions such as "What does _____ mean? Is there other evidence that supports that idea? Which side of the argument weighs more?"

Take a class poll to see which perspective was preferred by the pairs. Have a whole class discussion of the procedure: "Why do you suppose the decisions weren't unanimous in our class? What can we conclude about the event using the multiple sources and taking different perspectives?" The teacher emphasizes the importance of clarifying and supporting ideas.

## 3. Conclusions

Revisit the art to have a final discussion that draws conclusions and makes broader inferences about multiple perspectives. The final discussion begins with an opportunity for students to share the decisions and compromises from their paired conversations. The teacher then broadens the scope of the discussion, asking questions such as, "Why do you suppose the interpretations are different within groups and between groups? What can you conclude about an event using multiple sources and taking different perspectives?" The teacher encourages students to guide the discussion as much as possible, often asking, "What could you ask now to clarify or further support the idea just shared?" This moves ownership of discussion and idea formation into students' hands.

## 4. Concluding Activity

Students create either: (a) a drawing portraying the event from a perspective other than the one shown, (b) a written description of how they would paint or visually portray the same event as an artist or from a perspective other than the one shown, or (c) a written entry in a "newly discovered" journal from the perspective of a person connected to the event.

As an added group activity, students can create a tableau of the scene while other students ask historical questions.

After the lesson on Vercingetorix, a student might create a painting from the point of view of Julius Caesar in which Vercingetorix is not portrayed as a colorful hero. Another student might decide to write a journal entry in a chapter of *The Gallic Wars* as written by Vercingetorix. It might start with "My name is Vercingetorix and I fought Julius Caesar in the Gallic Wars. . . . What I think people should know is . . ."

As a class project, half of the students pose in front of a life-sized projected image of the painting. The other half of the class asks questions using the "Art Analysis" or "Document Analysis" questions. Students take on the role of the person they are posing as and answer the questions. Some students will portray Vercingetorix and his soldiers, some will be Caesar and his soldiers.

## Reflection Questions and Action Plans

### Reflection Questions

The past is difficult to retrieve. One must piece together a puzzle as one would do detective work. Some questions to consider when planning the lesson are:

- What works of art are there that relate to my topic?

- If in the textbook, why did the authors choose this particular work of art? What is the message it communicates?

- Does the textbook present multiple points of view?

- What other primary and secondary sources can I find representing the perspective of the textbook, opposing perspectives, and those perspectives absent from the textbook?

- How do we corroborate evidence?

### Action Plans

We have implemented this approach with great success using a variety of topics and employing both primary and secondary sources, including the textbook. You would first need to check the grade-level standards for history-social science and for the visual arts in your own state.

The topics that may be addressed through the arts are endless and include any art medium or style. Here are some additional topics and resource ideas for this pedagogical practice:

- "Washington Crossing the Delaware" (Leutze, 1851) and "Washington's Crossing: McKonkey's Ferry, Dec 26, 1776" (Küntsler, 2011) illustrate two different versions of the same event. These can be compared to several primary sources, such as the George Washington Papers (Library of Congress), The Journal of Col. John Fitzgerald, and The Journal of John Bostwick. Any textbook account can be used, such as DiBacco, Mason, and Appy's *History of the United States* (Houghton Mifflin, 1992).

- John Vanderlyn's painting "The Landing of Columbus" (1847) can be compared to Columbus's Log.

- "The Bloody Massacre in King-Street" engraving and text (1770) by Paul Revere can be compared to primary sources from testimony at the trial of Captain Preston.

- "Deacon Samuel Chapin" (1881), a sculpture also known as "The Puritan," by Augustus Saint-Gaudens, can be compared to accounts by John Winthrop, Mary Dwyer, and Anne Hutchinson.

- The "Death of Caesar" (1860), a painting by Jean-Leon Gerome, and Vincenzo Camuccini's painting "Death of Julius Caesar" (1798) can be compared to reports by Plutarch and Suetonius.

You can, of course, create your own activities using this pedagogical practice, depending on what you are teaching. Here are several steps that can help.

1. Use the topic of your unit as you look at history standards that you intend to teach. Develop several key questions that you want students to be able to answer, along with any historical thinking skills that you want them to hone during the lessons.

2. Gather a varied set of written primary and secondary sources that describe the event or topic, ideally from different perspectives and voices.

3. Search for artwork that depicts key events or ideas in the unit you are teaching. Even doing a basic image search online will often yield works of art and their titles that you can further explore.

4. Look for works of art that differ from each other and differ from other primary and secondary sources that you are using. Consider how analyzing and discussing the differences might be helpful for students to develop their understanding of what (likely) happened and to develop their historical thinking skills.

5. Develop lessons as described above in the model lesson for this chapter.

_____

Here is a summary list of the templates you may use during the lesson.

- Art Analysis Questions (Table 2)

- Analyzing an Image (Figure 2)

- Comparing Multiple Sources Graphic Organizer (Figure 3)

- Analyzing a Document (Table 3)

- Evidence Collection (Figure 4)

- Drawing Conclusions (Figure 5)

## References

Beardsley, E. (2013). How Gaul-ing: Celebrating France's first resistance fighter. *National Public Radio*. Retrieved from http://www.npr.org/2013/08/08/209514127/how-gaul-ing-celebrating-frances-first -resistance-fighter

Burstein, S. M., & Shek, R. (2006). From republic to empire. In *World history, ancient civilizations* (p. 353). Orlando, FL: Holt, Rinehart & Winston.

California State Board of Education. (1998). *History-social science content standards for California public schools: Kindergarten through grade twelve.* Sacramento, CA: Author.

California State Board of Education. (2001). *Visual and performing arts standards for California public schools: Pre-kindergarten through grade twelve.* Sacramento, CA: Author.

California State Board of Education. (2012). *English language development standards: Kindergarten through grade twelve.* Sacramento, CA: Author.

Crespin, L. (1998). Developing perceptual skills in art criticism. In J. Stern, *Painted light, California impressionist paintings* (pp. i–ii). Carson, CA: California State University Dominguez Hills, University Art Gallery.

Goldenberg, C., & Coleman, R. (2010) *Promoting academic achievement among English learners: A guide to the research.* Thousand Oaks, CA: Corwin Press.

Haywood, J. (2009). Vercingetorix and the failure of Gallic resistance. *History Today, 59*(9). Retrieved from http://www.historytoday.com/john-haywood/vercingetorix-and-failure-gallic-resistance

Hill, J., & Miller, K. (2013). *Classroom instruction that works with English language learners* (2nd ed.). Denver, CO: MCREL.

Hutton, L. (2014). *The history project.* Long Beach, CA: California State University, Long Beach & Dominguez Hills.

Kleinfelder, K. (1998). Questioning the work of art. In J. Stern, *Painted light, California impressionist paintings* (pp. iii–1). Carson, CA: California State University, Dominguez Hills, University Art Gallery.

Künstler, M. (2011). *Washington's crossing: McKonkey's ferry, Dec. 26, 1776* [painting]. Retrieved from: http://cityroom.blogs.nytimes.com/2011/12/23/a-famous-painting-meets-its-more-factual-match/

Leutze, E. G. (1851). *Washington crossing the Delaware* [painting]. New York, NY: The Metropolitan Museum of Art.

National Governors Association Center for Best Practices & Council of Chief State School Officers. (2010). *Common Core State Standards for English language arts & literacy in history/social studies, science, and technical subjects.* Washington, DC: Authors. Retrieved from: http://www.corestandards.org/ELA-Literacy/RH/6-8/

Royer, L. N. (1899). *Vercingetorix throws down his arms at the feet of Julius Caesar* [painting]. Retrieved from: http://www.historytoday.com/john-haywood/vercingetorix-and-failure-gallic-resistance

Rozenzweig, R., & Wineburg, S. (n.d.). Why historical thinking matters. Retrieved from http://historicalthinkingmatters.org/why.html

Schrum, K. (n.d.). What is historical thinking? Retrieved from http://teachinghistory.org/historical-thinking-intro

Siegenthaler, J. (Ed). (1999). *Looking at history through art.* Los Angeles, CA: Los Angeles County Museum of Art.

Soto-Hinman, I. (2011). Increasing academic oral language development: Using English language learner shadowing in classrooms. *Multicultural Education, 18*(2), 21–23.

Stokstad, M. (2005). *Art history* (2nd ed.). Upper Saddle River, NJ: Pearson Prentice Hall.

Suh, Y. (2013). Past looking: Using arts as historical evidence in teaching history. *Social Studies Research and Practice, 8*(1), 135–159. Retrieved from http://www.socstrpr.org/wp-content/uploads/2013/09/MS06372Spring2013.pdf

Wineburg, S. (2001). *Historical thinking and other unnatural acts: Charting the future of teaching the past.* Philadelphia, PA: Temple University Press.

Zwiers, J., O'Hara, S., & Pritchard, R. (2014). *Common Core standards in diverse classrooms: Essential practices for developing academic language and disciplinary literacy.* Portland, ME: Stenhouse.

# SCIENCE AND
# TECHNICAL SUBJECTS

# Engaging in Phenomena From Project-Based Learning in a Place-Based Context in Science

*Okhee Lee, New York University*

*Emily Miller, University of Wisconsin–Madison*

Integration of language and content, including science, has been called for for all students, and this is a challenge for ELLs in particular, who are tasked to learn the content in the language they are still developing. This call has become a policy initiative with direct impact on classroom teaching through the Common Core State Standards (CCSS) for English Language Arts (ELA) & Literacy in History/Social Studies, Science, and Technical Subjects (National Governors Association Center for Best Practices [NGA] & Council of Chief State School Officers [CCSSO], 2010a), on the one hand, and the Next Generation Science Standards (NGSS; NGSS Lead States, 2013a), on the other hand. The NGSS became public in 2013, while implementation of the CCSS has been underway since adoption starting in 2010.

The CCSS emphasize literacy in history/social studies, science, and technical subjects for Grades 6–12 as follows:

> The grades 6–12 standards are divided into two sections, one for ELA and the other for history/social studies, science, and technical subjects. This division reflects the unique, time-honored place of ELA teachers in developing students' literacy skills while at the same time recognizing that teachers in other areas must have a role in this development as well.
>
> Part of the motivation behind the interdisciplinary approach to literacy promulgated by the Standards is extensive research establishing the need for college and career ready students to be proficient in reading complex informational text independently in a variety of content areas. Most of the required reading in college and workforce training programs is informational in structure and challenging in content; postsecondary education programs typically

provide students with both a higher volume of such reading than is generally required in K–12 schools and comparatively little scaffolding. (NGA & CCSSO, 2010a, p. 4)

In the NGSS, "every effort has been made to ensure consistency between the CCSS and the NGSS" (NGSS Lead States, 2013b, p. 1). While connections to the CCSS for ELA are included across all grade levels/bands in the NGSS, connections for Grades 6–12 are highlighted in the NGSS Appendix M (2013b):

Literacy skills are critical to building knowledge in science. To ensure the CCSS literacy standards work in tandem with the specific content demands outlined in the NGSS, the NGSS development team worked with the CCSS writing team to identify key literacy connections to the specific content demands outlined in the NGSS. (p. 1)

In this chapter, we address the CCSS for literacy in science for ELLs in Grades 6–12. We highlight three key ideas. First, we describe how the CCSS, interwoven with the NGSS, present ELLs with learning opportunities and demands in both language and science. Second, we focus on specific demands as well as opportunities that ELLs may experience as they engage in argumentation. Third, for pedagogical practice, we combine components of project-based learning (engaging in phenomena) with place-based learning. The classroom vignette illustrates learning opportunities and demands in language and science for middle-school ELLs.

## The Common Core State Standards and Specific Demands for ELLs

The CCSS for ELA and literacy offer "a portrait of students who meet the standards set out in this document" (NGA & CCSSO, 2010a, p. 7). The CCSS further state, "As students advance through the grades and master the standards in reading, writing, speaking, listening, and language, they are able to exhibit with increasing fullness and regularity these capacities of the literate individual" (p. 7). The seven capacities or practices for ELA and literacy include:

1. Demonstrate independence

2. Build strong content knowledge

3. Respond to the varying demands of audience, task, purpose, and discipline

4. Comprehend as well as critique

5. Value evidence

6. Use technology and digital media strategically and capably

7. Come to understand other perspectives and cultures (p. 7)

In a similar manner, "A Framework for K–12 Science Education: Practices, Crosscutting Concepts, and Core Ideas" (National Research Council, 2012), from which the NGSS were developed, highlight science and engineering practices. The framework emphasizes "developing students' proficiency in science in a coherent way across grades K–12 following the logic of learning progressions" (p. 33). The eight science and engineering practices include:

1. Ask questions (for science) and define problems (for engineering)

2. Develop and use models

3. Plan and carry out investigations

4. Analyze and interpret data

5. Use mathematics and computational thinking

6. Construct explanations (for science) and design solutions (for engineering)

7. Engage in argument from evidence

8. Obtain, evaluate, and communicate information (p. 3)

Science and engineering practices are language intensive, and engagement in these practices requires science classroom discourse (CCSSO, 2012; Lee, Quinn, & Valdés, 2013). Students speak and listen as they present their ideas or engage in reasoned argumentation with others to refine their ideas and reach shared conclusions. They read, write, view, and visually represent as they develop their models and explanations. These practices offer rich opportunities and demands for language learning at the same time as they promote science learning.

This chapter highlights three key ideas. First, across the CCSS and NGSS, these new standards share a common emphasis on disciplinary practices and classroom discourse. These practices raise the bar for content (academically rigorous), raise the bar for language (language intensive), and call for a high level of classroom discourse. Because the CCSS and NGSS are academically rigorous, teachers should make instructional shifts to enable all students to be college and career ready. At the same time, because disciplinary practices in the CCSS and NGSS are language intensive, teachers should address increased language demands while capitalizing on language learning opportunities across these subject areas for all students. Furthermore, teachers should engage all students, including ELLs, in rich classroom discourse in oral and written forms.

Second, we focus on the CCSS capacities 4 and 5: comprehend as well as critique, and value evidence. The CCSS Anchor Standards focus heavily on argument, involving claim, evidence, and reasoning across grade levels. Not only are these CCSS capacities and Anchor Standards critical for ELA and literacy, but they overlap with the NGSS science and engineering practice 7: engage in argument from evidence. (Note: The CCSS for ELA and literacy and the NGSS also overlap with the CCSS for mathematical practice 3: construct viable arguments and critique the reasoning of others [NGA & CCSSO, 2010c, p. 6], but this chapter does not address the CCSS for mathematics.)

Third, in connecting the CCSS to science instruction with all students and ELLs in particular, we propose pedagogical practice that combines components of project-based learning (engaging in phenomena) with place-based learning. Through project-based learning, students are immersed in investigating a driving question to explain a phenomenon or design solutions to a problem through collaborative activities (Krajcik & Czerniak, 2013). Through place-based learning, students are immersed in local contexts of homes and communities (Smith, 2002; Sobel, 2005). In the science classroom, students make sense of phenomena or problems (components of project-based learning) in local contexts of homes and communities (place-based learning). The focus on making sense of a phenomenon or problem in a place-based context presents opportunities and demands for both science learning and language learning with all students, including ELLs. Specifically, we highlight how ELLs engage in argument from evidence as they explain a phenomenon or design a solution to a problem in their home and community context.

# Rationale

Pedagogical practice of engaging in phenomena in a place-based context combines components of project-based learning and place-based learning. In this section, after a brief description of project-based learning and place-based learning, we explain how and why this pedagogical practice helps teachers address both the CCSS and NGSS with ELLs, specifically the language and science demands as ELLs engage in argumentation from evidence. We highlight that although the pedagogical practice is effective for all students, it is particularly effective for ELLs.

## Project-Based Learning and Place-Based Learning

Project-based learning is an approach that immerses students in driving questions, investigations, and collaboration to explain phenomena in the natural world and develop solutions to problems in the designed world. Project-based learning is based on six design features (Krajcik & Czerniak, 2013):

1. Learning goals driven

2. Focus on making sense of meaningful phenomena and solving real-world problems

3. Collaborative activities to explore driving questions

4. Creation of products that address driving questions

5. Use of learning technologies as tools

6. Scaffolds or more knowledgeable others supporting learners with complex tasks

Although each of the above design features is essential in project-based learning, we highlight *focus on making sense of meaningful phenomena and solving real world problems*, which allows access for ELLs in learning science. The phenomenon or the problem connects students to academically rigorous ideas in science and engineering, as they figure out explanations for the phenomenon or solutions to the problem over an extended period of time. In addition, collaborative sense making is language intensive, as students communicate their ideas, argue about the credibility of ideas, and revise their explanations and solutions based on new evidence.

Place-based learning structures learning around culture, language, environment, local history, and economy (see Avery, 2013, for details):

Place-based education uses the local environment as a starting point to teach subjects including language arts, mathematics, social studies, and science. Emphasizing hands-on, real-world learning experiences, this approach increases academic achievement, strengthens students' ties to their community, enhances students' appreciation for the natural world, and creates a heightened commitment to serving as contributing citizens. (Sobel, 2005, p. 7)

Smith (2002) emphasizes that place-based education emerges from a specific place that includes cultural and nature studies from that place, connects students with the community and involves them in decision-making and real-world problem solving, and bridges the gap between their local knowledge and school science. Thus, the literature indicates that a place-based context allows students to learn science across local contexts of school, home, and community that capitalize on their everyday language and experience, including ELLs' home language and culture. A place-based context shows students that science is rooted in their daily lives.

## Learning Opportunities and Demands for Science and Language With ELLs

Pedagogical practice of engaging in a phenomenon from project-based learning in a place-based context presents learning opportunities and demands for both science and language with ELLs (Lee, Quinn, & Valdés, 2013; Miller & Krajcik, 2015). An engaging phenomenon from project-based learning offers various entry points for science and language learning with ELLs. In addition, relating the phenomenon to a place-based context of ELLs' home and community allows them to build on their prior knowledge, including home language and culture. Furthermore, engaging in a phenomenon in a place-based context provides opportunities for authentic and meaningful discourse through engagement in science and engineering practices with appropriate language supports.

Although the CCSS for literacy in science and technical subjects as well as history/social studies include standards only for reading and writing (NGA & CCSSO, 2010a, pp. 59–66), we emphasize that oral discourse through listening and speaking is critical for collaborative sense-making for both science and language learning. Oral discourse is particularly important with ELLs:

> This focus on oral language is of greatest importance for the children most at risk—children for whom English is a second language and children who have not been exposed at home to the kind of language found in written texts (Dickinson & Smith, 1994). Ensuring that all children in the United States have access to an excellent education requires that issues of oral language come to the fore in elementary classrooms. (NGA & CCSSO, 2010b, p. 27)

## Argument From Evidence

As ELLs try to figure out the phenomenon, they engage in argument with evidence based on observations and data (NGSS science and engineering practice 7); comprehend as well as critique, and value evidence based on science texts and discourse (CCSS capacities 4 and 5); and meet the CCSS Anchor Standards focusing on argumentation that involves claim, reasoning, and evidence. In ELA, evidence is drawn from texts, both literary and informational. While reading, a student critically weighs a range of evidence drawn from texts and an author's reasoning. While writing, a student considers what evidence best fits the particular task at hand with audience and purpose in mind. In science, evidence is based on data, including both laboratory and field observations, about a phenomenon or system. As students advance through the grades, they gain facility with various uses of evidence across subject areas.

While students use various modalities of language through speaking and listening (oral), reading and writing (written), and viewing representing (visual), we emphasize oral discourse for collaborative sense-making. As students engage in argument, they rely heavily on oral discourse in small or large group settings. Students discuss their observations and engage in argument using evidence with others in small groups until they reach a shared "best" explanation or model. After small groups of students make oral presentations of their results and conclusions, they engage in discourse with other students who ask questions and discuss issues raised in the presentations. Because the oral discourse of such presentations and discussions is different from their everyday discourse, scientific arguments in oral forms precede in written forms. More typically, the development of both oral and written forms of scientific arguments proceeds in parallel.

In this section, we have offered the rationale for how and why the pedagogical practice of engaging in phenomena in a place-based context helps teachers address both the language and science demands as ELLs engage in argumentation from evidence. In the next section, we present a classroom vignette of ELLs engaging in phenomena from project-based learning in a place-based context across life and physical science disciplines in middle school.

## Pedagogical Practice: Engaging in Phenomena From Project-Based Learning in a Place-Based Context

This vignette describes a science unit in middle school (MS) that aligns to performance expectations (or standards) in life science (LS2-2) and physical science (PS1-4). The instruction took place in a medium sized shipbuilding and port city in the Midwest.

- Construct an explanation that predicts patterns of interactions among organisms across multiple ecosystems. (MS LS2-2)

- Develop a model that predicts and describes changes in particle motion, temperature, and state of a pure substance when thermal energy is added or removed. (MS PS1-4)

In addition, the vignette addresses the CCSS for literacy in science, with a focus on the Anchor Standard Integration of Knowledge and Ideas under Reading Standards for Literacy in Science and Technical Subjects 6–12 (NGA & CCSSO, 2010a, p. 62):

- Integrate quantitative or technical information expressed in words in a text with a version of that information expressed visually (e.g., in a flowchart, diagram, model, graph, or table). (RST.6–8.7)

- Distinguish among facts, reasoned judgment based on research findings, and speculation in a text. (RST.6–8.8)

- Compare and contrast the information gained from experiments, simulations, video, or multimedia sources with that gained from reading a text on the same topic. (RST.6–8.9)

The vignette highlights three key ideas emphasized in this chapter. While the vignette is organized into two sections on the first two key ideas, the third idea is embedded throughout the vignette.

1) The use of an engaging phenomenon in a place-based context is key to supporting ELLs' engagement and discourse. The phenomenon itself—an invasion of a local lake by a harmful zooplankton—is the scaffold that the teacher relies on to foster meaning making. The numerous avenues he employs to build more complex and increasingly nuanced meaning from the phenomenon are illustrated.

2) The CCSS and the NGSS emphasize the practice of argumentation in terms of supporting and substantiating claims based on reasoning and evidence, but science takes this practice of argumentation further. Scientists seek to create scenarios where the claim is tested and either refuted or supported using observations or data in evaluation of the claim. In the vignette, the teacher pushes the students to analyze each other's claims critically in light of the evidence and reasoning, but also in terms of accuracy of science knowledge.

3) As students try to make sense of a phenomenon in a place-based context, they experience learning opportunities and demands in science and language. With support from the teacher and peers, ELLs at varying levels of proficiency successfully engage in argumentation about the phenomenon in the context of home, community, and school.

## Vignette
### Students Engage in a Phenomenon in a Place-Based Context

Mr. Edelstein's 7th-grade science class discovered that their science field trip was a walk to nearby Lake Michigan. The lake was beginning to look more like a soupy pond in places where the waves met the shore. There were a dozen dead fish in various stages of decomposition and a thick carpet of algae. Mr. Edelstein led the students straight to the dead fish amid loud protests from students. "What's this?"

Mr. Edelstein asked everyone the first driving question of the unit: "Why do we have all these dead fish at our lake?"

"Alright!" Edrissa said with excitement, "Now that's what I'm talking about!" He leaned over, identified the fish as smelt, and dramatically took a step back. The smelt was really weird looking. It looked as though the middle-sized fish had been feeding on darning needles and safety pins. Small spikes jutted out of the fish's stomach and made weird-shaped bulges. The teacher asked students to talk with their assigned small group partners. What had happened to the smelt?

Rosalie said confidently, "It had something wrong with it. Probably a disease." She paused, "And the fish, it is definitely long dead."

Vanessa nodded, "Probably. She looks alien. The fish has this big tumor."

Adrian had a different opinion, "The stomach tumor, no." He pointed to his own stomach, "The fish, she . . . *nunca he visto*. She ate a, how you say, ate . . . very bad krilling, or . . . particulars." Rosalie and Vanessa saw that Adrian was right, the pokey things were in the stomach area and by the mouth.

The group of the above four students were at different levels of English proficiency. Adrian and Vanessa spoke Spanish as their home language. Vanessa, originally from Mexico, was an ELL at English language proficiency (ELP) level 3. Adrian, also from Mexico and a year in the United States, was an ELL at ELP level 2. Edrissa, a native English speaker, is African American. Rosalie, also a native English speaker, is Caucasian. (Note: All the names are pseudonyms.)

About half of the students in Mr. Edelstein's 7th-grade 55-minute science block love to fish. Edrissa fishes so often that he is considered the fishing expert of the class. Vanessa has a lot of experience fishing with her family in the small lakes around the city. Adrian has fished a few times. Students who do not fish, like Rosalie, have heard of the spiny water flea because of the community's shipbuilding and sport fishing economy.

Edrissa joined Adrian, Rosalie, and Vanessa and shared his thoughts about the strange looking smelt with his group and the class, "I think all of this disgusting *disgustingness* is because of the spiny water flea. It makes the lake green and kills fish. I still fish here sometimes, TBH [to be honest], but mostly go to Aniwa Lake." Some of the students had already encountered the spiny water flea. They had seen marshmallow-like blobs midway on their fishing lines, and juvenile fish with the 1-cm long crustaceans' jagged spines lodged in the mouths. Adrian said to his group, "I catched a big fish and see the fish eating that . . . on the mouth."

"Did you let it go?" asked Vanessa.

Adrian said, "I let it go, the fish."

Mr. Edelstein told the students that their job was the same as scientists. The students were going to predict which of two very different lakes, Lake Vilas or Lake Aniwa, could become invaded by the spiny water flea. They would be creating a class video to inform the community members how to keep the "invader" from spreading to that lake. He said that only six of the state's 16,000 lakes had been invaded so far, but the spiny water flea was found in Lake Michigan and scientists were worried it would spread throughout the state. "First, we need to know more about the spiny water flea," he announced, "and also a lot more about these two lakes."

Mr. Edelstein's instructions for the small student groups were to discuss and ask questions about what was happening in Lake Michigan. They needed to (a) locate specified items (dead fish, algae, lake water, macrophytes, and, if possible, spiny water flea, and Daphnia); (b) photograph or sketch the items using iPads; (c) agree upon and record descriptions of the items; and (d) discuss and record the features of the lake. The group consisting of Adrian, Edrissa, Rosalie, and Vanessa decided that the best way to describe the spiny water flea was "white mosquito." They needed to discern the shape and deepness of the lake, the lake's productivity (level of organic activity in the lake), and water input and output. They also recorded the water temperature. Last, they used their iPad to create a short video of the shore, the status of the invasion of the spiny water flea, and their initial thoughts.

The activity—looking for items, taking pictures and videos, and describing and discussing the invasive species event—immersed Adrian and Vanessa, both ELLs with emerging proficiency in English, in the focus of study. Because the phenomenon was a shared experience in the classroom and in the community, they became acquainted with the science topic and began initial meaning making around the topic in English.

The day after visiting the lake, back in the classroom, the students shared fishing stories (netting smelt, avoiding sheephead) and discussed what their families had answered to the homework question, "What makes lakes get algae?" At home, some students had talked about these questions with family in languages other than English. These discussions in home languages about place-based topics offered leverage for the ELLs to build on linguistic and cultural resources. They connected school science with home and community, which fueled their understanding.

Mr. Edelstein solicited student-initiated questions to give rise to the driving question for investigation. The student groups reviewed their data in videos, photos, and texts, and wrote down questions. Each group selected questions to share with the class, and Mr. Edelstein wrote them down on the white board. Some questions were about Lake Michigan: "Does the spiny water flea make the algae?" and, "What else does the spiny water flea do to Lake Michigan?" Some questions were about other lakes: "Will the spiny water flea get into Lake Aniwa or Lake Vilas, or both?" and "Will it like one lake more than the other?" And some questions were about the spiny water flea: "How can such a tiny, almost invisible thing, cause so much *stress*?" Mr. Edelstein said that the students would be figuring out the second driving question of the unit:

"Will the spiny water flea more likely thrive in Lake Aniwa or Lake Vilas?"

Although the class couldn't take a field trip to Lake Aniwa or Lake Vilas, they collected and examined photos and maps of the lakes. Mr. Edelstein videotaped himself measuring the temperature and collecting data about the lakes' features. He shared the videos with the class, who recorded the new information on their shared small group iPad data collection page. Lake Vilas had no algae and no dead fish. Lake Aniwa was much warmer than Lake Vilas.

The class needed to figure out how the two lakes were different from Lake Michigan, and how those differences determine which environments were suitable for the spiny water flea. They studied topographical maps of all three lakes and created 3D models. The class made use of and built on the language they had developed on the first day when describing the features of Lake Michigan. Aided by the photos and the videos they had taken, they constructed ideas using more accurate and precise language to compare the two lakes with Lake Michigan. For example, Lake Vilas was narrower and had steeper slopes than Lake Michigan, whereas Lake Aniwa was shallower and wider. Lake Vilas was fed by cold groundwater flow, whereas Lake Aniwa had surface water flow.

To understand the effects of these differences, Mr. Edelstein made a model of convection using a beaker, food coloring, and a hot plate. He then asked students, in small groups, to investigate how changes in temperature affect the particle movement of water. The students used food coloring to model the water particle movement in Lakes Aniwa and Lake Vilas. In a shallow beaker blown by a hair dryer to represent warm air temperatures mixing with water in Lake Aniwa, the water mixed constantly. But in the tall beaker with ice under the bottom to represent the cold ground water input of Lake Vilas, only the top layer mixed. The students in small groups drew models to explain the differences in layers of temperatures, and the mixing of these layers, between the two lakes. They used the topographical maps, the models, and the videos and photos of the features of Lake Michigan and the other two lakes as sources of evidence to support their discussion.

Mr. Edelstein had collected two types of zooplankton in the lakes: the invasive spiny water flea and the native Daphnia. In the days that followed, the students observed the zooplankton under microscopes and modeled the life cycles of the crustaceans, and how these life cycles correspond to the changing feeding habits of growing fish. The spiny water flea clones itself when resources are plentiful, and only sexually reproduces under stressful conditions. The groups used their iPad photos and sketches from the first day to create food webs. Many of the students shared that the walleye, bass, and northern pike eat minnows, which in turn eat Daphnia. The Daphnia eat algae. So when there are many Daphnia, the algae is kept in check.

Mr. Edelstein placed on the overhead a graph from a research paper about Lake Michigan and the clarity of water before and after invasion. He used the students' collected samples of water, with their short written descriptions of the items from the first day, to construct shared meaning around the discussion of the graph. The graph showed that after invasion of the spiny water flea, the population of Daphnia was depleted and algae flourished. Edrissa said, "I think the graph showing contamination in the water pre- and postinfestation, it means that Lake Aniwa would get more spiny water flea because it has all the algae."

Vanessa disagreed. She argued, "It's obviously that I can see more water—no—more deep of this lake preinfestation. After infestation I cannot see more deep water."

Edrissa said, "I don't get it. Why is that evidence that the spiny water flea would be success-ful—that there is *less* algae?"

Vanessa picked up a vial of Daphnia and used the word "crash," the academic term introduced by the graph for population reduction: "Because the Daphnia is eating the algae. Too much algae, and the algae-grazer is crashing too much."

Rosalie added, "Vanessa means that lots of algae shows that Daphnia are missing in the lake!"

Adrian pointed to the group's hand-drawn trophic pyramid, which added another major conse-quence in the microecosystem. He said, "The big, big fish, it's gonna die because his food it's die, because *his* food die."

Edrissa nodded glumly, "It's a disaster. They would be most successful where everything is already balanced."

Vanessa and Edrissa both used the same graph that compared water clarity in the fall before and after invasion as evidence for their conflicting claims. Vanessa reasoned differently from Edrissa that an invasion of the spiny water flea was more likely in the deep lake with less algae than in the shal-low lake with more algae. She reasoned a cause and effect relationship between the two correlated variables. Despite the challenging task of sense making, the group was engaged and persevered in understanding Vanessa's idea. Rosalie and Adrian clarified and extended Vanessa's idea for the group.

## Students Engage in Argumentation Through Claim, Evidence, and Reasoning

After 3 weeks of study, Edrissa's group placed their scientific explanation next to another group's explanation. The two groups were to critically respond to each other's explanation. As instructed by Mr. Edelstein, the students wrote their claims using a Claims, Evidence and Reasoning template. Edrissa's group came to the following explanation:

The spiny water flea can survive in Lake Vilas and not in Lake Aniwa. (claim) Lake Vilas has almost no algae and Lake Aniwa has a lot. This is important because in lakes where there is less algae, there is likely more Daphnia. We saw in the microscope that Daphnia eat algae, and spiny water flea eat Daphnia, and spiny water fleas do not eat algae [evidence]. In order for animals to survive they must have energy, which Daphnia can get from food algae and spiny water flea get from Daphnia. If animals do not get their energy they will die (reason-ing). Lakes where there is more algae, there is less Daphnia living there to eat it. The spiny water flea survive only where there is Daphnia because they eat Daphnia (reasoning).

The neighboring group discussed this explanation and whether the evidence and reasoning was sufficient. One student said, "It's true, when you see no algae then Daphnia has grazed there. And Lake Vilas is the most similar to Lake Michigan, and we know they like Lake Michigan already."

Another student brought up an interesting point, "But we investigated Daphnia and watched them eat the piece of algae. They have to have algae to live, and no algae might just mean there never was algae in the lake, and so there would be no food for the Daphnia. At all. The spiny water flea would not survive without food."

Mr. Edelstein asked a question of Edrissa's group, "Could you test your claim? How?"

Adrian answered hesitantly, "We can put a little algae. If we see the *Daphnia* eating that . . ."

Vanessa answered at the same time, "We could just check for *Daphnia* in Vilas Lake!"

It is noted that the evidence and reasoning that Edrissa's group used to support their claim seemed sound. They used substantial evidence from the labs and a graph handout, seemingly sufficient evidence paired with logical reasoning. However, the explanation was scientifically inaccurate. The group suggested that the absence of algae indicated the presence of Daphnia, organisms that consume algae. They supported this claim because, in the graph, the presence of algae in Lake Michigan corresponded with a crash in the Daphnia population, and the absence of algae occurred when Daphnia were present consumers. Yet, they had not considered another possibility that the absence of algae in Lake Vilas could also indicate that neither algae nor the Daphnia were present. Mr. Edelstein asked the students how they would test their claim, making their problematic logic clear.

Next, Edrissa's group was expected to react to their neighboring group's explanation with critical analysis. The neighboring group came to the same conclusion that Lake Vilas was more at risk, but they used different evidence and reasoning:

Lake Vilas is more likely to have spiny water fleas than Lake Aniwa because it is deep and narrow and Lake Aniwa is shallow, wide and deep and narrow lakes are best for spiny water fleas (claim). We know this because in the model and the maps, Lake Vilas is a very deep, clear lake with cold thermal layers and Lake Aniwa is shallow and warm, with no cold layers. We saw the life cycle that all of the spiny water flea survive and have eggs in cold clear water and they don't all live in warm water (evidence). Because of low temperature for their eggs and seeing their prey, and because the shape doesn't make much sediments and heat mixing, deeper lake is the best for the spiny water flea. Two things make a lake have cold layers, one is hydrologic inputs for water flow and the other is lake types. The lake type has to do with shape, and the shape of the Lake Vilas makes it mix only two times a year, and the shape of Lake Aniwa makes it always mixing (reasoning).

After the group read the text together, Edrissa faced the group and spoke up first. He was curious about the group's evidence about the spiny water flea's eggs in cold water. He said that when the spiny water flea had enough to eat and the water was an ideal temperature, it cloned itself; but when it didn't have enough food or the right temperature, it sexually reproduced. He asked, "What is best for survival? Is cloning better because it takes less energy?"

Vanessa and Rosalie listened to Edrissa and whispered together. Then they argued that Lake Aniwa could actually get more spiny water flea because it was *less* hospitable. Vanessa started emphatically, holding up her group's life cycle model of the spiny water flea, "I *totally* changed my mind. Here, the spiny water flea is so comfortable. She puts out 10 clones, two weeks, 10 clones, two weeks, 10 clones . . . The lake is *desbordado* . . . It's when the water lake it's up, she reproduces sexually. She is more . . . different . . . more successful."

Mr. Edelstein supplied, "more genetically different?"

Rosalie agreed with Vanessa and added, "Remember, yes, our life cycles, they are evidence to the opposite claim! Happy spiny water fleas clone. Just like that article about cloned bananas, clones can be weak. It is better for the spiny water flea to *sexually reproduce*, like . . . it does when it is not happy, because then it does not get too weak and die out, and more variety!"

Vanessa offered her argumentation that was scientifically accurate. Cloning, although efficient, causes the population to be weak. In contrast, the spiny water flea sexually reproduce when there is not enough food. They become genetically diverse, making them more resilient. Despite her emerging proficiency in English, Vanessa demonstrated complex reasoning with scientific accuracy that helped other students to explain the phenomenon that guided the entire unit.

Mr. Edelstein was pleased with Vanessa and Rosalie's argument and brought up the topic to discuss first in partners and then as a whole group. Students argued both sides, using the evidence collected and shown around the room. Mr. Edelstein reminded students that scientists were investigating a lot of these questions right now, as well. He asked the class to think about how a scientist could test the claim that a more genetically diverse population would be a greater threat to the ecosystem.

Adrian, Edrissa, Rosalie, and Vanessa agreed to make their educational video about precautions for the spiny water flea in the state's lakes. Together, the group used their video to warn other students in the school and families about the importance of drying boats and equipment when travelling from lake to lake. They decided to make one video in English and one in Spanish, because the people in the community spoke both languages.

Throughout the instruction, the evidence the students utilized for their argumentation came from funds of knowledge, the community setting, and in-class investigations. While engaging in argumentation, they used language in various oral and written forms. They created oral and written texts and used evidence and reasoning to engage critically in those texts. Adrian and Vanessa, both ELLs, were pivotal in making sense of the phenomenon with their group, shaping the group's knowledge, and producing the final group project of the educational video in both English and Spanish.

## Conclusion

The CCSS and the NGSS emphasize integration of language and content. The CCSS stress literacy in science and other subjects, while the NGSS make connections to the CCSS. Both the CCSS and the NGSS point out the importance of language and content integration for Grades 6–12 specifically. The CCSS and the NGSS, respectively and collectively, require instructional shifts with all students and ELLs in particular.

We have highlighted three key ideas in this chapter. First, the pedagogical practice of engaging in phenomena from project-based learning (Krajcik & Czerniak, 2013) in a place-based context (Smith, 2002; Sobel, 2005) scaffolds both language learning and science learning with ELLs. In the vignette, during a science field trip to nearby Lake Michigan, students observed dead fish in various stages of decomposition and a thick carpet of algae. To make sense of this phenomenon, the teacher introduced the driving question: "Why do we have all these dead fish at our lake?" As the unit progressed, students' investigations of the phenomenon generated the subsequent driving question: "Will the spiny water flea survive in Lake Aniwa or Lake Vilas?" As the phenomenon occurred in a shared space of home and community settings, the teacher used the notion of place and students' expertise with their prior science knowledge as a scaffold for meaning making. Furthermore, the shared space of home and community settings supported ELLs to use a shared language via home language and English.

Second, the CCSS and the NGSS emphasize disciplinary practices, which are language intensive and require a high level of classroom discourse (CCSSO, 2012; Lee, Quinn, & Valdés, 2013). In particular, both the CCSS and the NGSS highlight the practice of argumentation from evidence. In the vignette, ELLs were immersed and invested in the phenomenon at hand and lent their expertise and community-based knowledge to make sense of the phenomenon and construct increasingly complex ideas through making claims, providing evidence, and communicating their reasoning. The final group project to produce an educational video was responsive to a real-world problem in the community.

Third, the CCSS and the NGSS present both learning opportunities and demands in language and science. As a case in point, the practice of argumentation from evidence is academically rigorous and language intensive. In the vignette, the teacher supported ELLs to meet increased language demands while capitalizing on language learning opportunities. Students were immersed in multimodal, multisensory, and interactive modes of discourse in various oral and written forms across small group and whole class settings. As they tried to make sense of the phenomenon, they used multiple languages, including home language and English. Language is used for function and action (Van Lier & Walqui, 2012), which presents a contrast to a more traditional approach to second language acquisition that focuses on discrete elements of vocabulary and grammar.

## Reflection Questions and Action Plans

### Reflection Questions

The reflection questions address how the pedagogical practice of engaging in phenomena from project-based learning in a place-based context is highlighted in the vignette. Specifically, the questions focus on argumentation from evidence as highlighted in the CCSS and the NGSS:

- What were some ways that the teacher used the phenomenon as a scaffold for learning language and science?

- How did the teacher utilize the place of students' home and community to engage them in learning language and science?

- What example(s) in the vignette indicate when students' explanations were scientifically inaccurate, although the evidence and reasoning seemed logical? How was this discrepancy resolved?

- How did the teacher's purposeful attention to collaborative group work promote learning language and science?

- How were the two small groups supported in analyzing and critiquing each other's explanations?

- How did the final group project of producing educational videos for the community lend authenticity to doing science and using language?

## Action Plans

The action plans include recommended tasks and activities for teachers to apply the ideas presented both within and outside their classrooms. These recommendations are illustrated in the vignette.

1. The phenomenon to guide science instruction should be engaging to students. Furthermore, a phenomenon should be engaging enough to sustain students' interest throughout the unit.

   a. A phenomenon is powerful when it is a local event that is shared among students and relevant to their lives at home and community. The importance of a shared experience that scaffolds meaning making cannot be underscored. Carefully plan what this phenomenon will be and how it will be leveraged.

   b. For ELLs, a shared experience in home and community settings invites use of home languages as a scaffold for meaning making. For ELLs, consider a phenomenon that the students have experience in, so they can be leaders in shaping the discussion. This also sets the stage for other students to seek out ELLs' expertise.

2. Teachers need to hone their place-based science knowledge. They must be invested in culling the current science understandings, on the one hand, and the questions and concerns in the community, on the other hand. To communicate this critical relationship between the science and the community, teachers must present that investment as another member of the community.

3. In supporting students to engage in argumentation from evidence in the science classroom, teachers need to attend to accuracy of science knowledge in the reasoning process. Science has a canon of accepted knowledge that explains how the natural world works, which is often inconsistent with students' preconceptions. An idea that seems sound logically may not be accurate scientifically. Teachers use this situation as an important opportunity to construct new understandings.

4. In the science classroom, language is being used for function and action (Van Lier & Walqui, 2012), that is, making meaning of science. When supported appropriately, most ELLs are capable of learning science "through their emerging language and of comprehending and carrying out sophisticated language functions (e.g., arguing from

evidence, providing explanations) using less-than-perfect English" (Lee, Quinn, & Valdés, 2013, p. 227). Teachers engage ELLs in disciplinary practices of ELA and science to promote both science knowledge and language proficiency.

5. Students' ideas can be translated to videos and to texts, which can be leveraged for learning. Student-created videos and texts can be used to help the students gradually attend to precision and accuracy of language. Students must learn to clarify each other's words, and to critique and challenge these texts.

## References

Avery, L. M. (2013). Rural science education: Valuing local knowledge. *Theory Into Practice, 52*(1), 28–35.

Council of Chief State School Officers. (2012). *Framework for English language proficiency development standards corresponding to the Common Core State Standards and the Next Generation Science Standards.* Washington, DC: Author.

Krajcik, J. S., & Czerniak, C. (2013). *Teaching science in elementary and middle school classrooms: A project-based approach* (4th ed.). London, England: Routledge.

Lee, O., Quinn, H., & Valdés, G. (2013). Science and language for English language learners in relation to Next Generation Science Standards and with implications for Common Core State Standards for English language arts and mathematics. *Educational Researcher, 42*(4), 223–233.

Miller, E., & Krajcik, J. (2015). Reflecting on instruction to promote equity and alignment to the NGSS. In O. Lee, E. Miller, & R. Januszyk (Eds.), *NGSS for all students* (pp. 179–188). Arlington, VA: National Science Teachers Association.

National Governors Association Center for Best Practices & Council of Chief State School Officers. (2010a). *Common Core State Standards for English language arts and literacy in history/social studies, science, and technical subjects.* Washington, DC: Authors.

National Governors Association Center for Best Practices & Council of Chief State School Officers. (2010b). *Common Core State Standards for English language arts & literacy in history/social studies, science, and technical subjects. Appendix A: Research supporting key elements of the standards.* Washington, DC: Authors. Retrieved from http://www.corestandards.org/assets/Appendix_A.pdf

National Governors Association Center for Best Practices & Council of Chief State School Officers. (2010c). *Common Core State Standards for mathematics.* Washington, DC: Authors.

National Research Council. (2012). *A framework for K–12 science education: Practices, crosscutting concepts, and core ideas.* Washington, DC: National Academies Press.

NGSS Lead States. (2013a). *Next Generation Science Standards: For states, by states.* Washington, DC: The National Academies Press.

NGSS Lead States. (2013b). *Next Generation Science Standards: For states, by states: Appendix M—Connections to the Common Core State Standards for literacy in science and technical subjects.* Retrieved from http://www.nextgenscience.org/sites/ngss/files/Appendix%20M%20Connections%20to%20the%20CCSS%20for%20Literacy_061213.pdf

Smith, G. (2002). Place-based education: Learning to be where we are. *Phi Delta Kappan, 83,* 584–594.

Sobel, D. (2005). *Place-based education: Connecting classrooms & communities.* Great Barrington, MA: Orion Society.

Van Lier, L., & Walqui, A. (2012). Language and the Common Core State Standards. Understanding language: Language, literacy, and learning in the content areas. Retrieved from http://ell.stanford.edu/sites/default/files/pdf/academic-papers/04-Van Lier Walqui Language and CCSS FINAL.pdf

# Writing to Achieve the Common Core State Standards in Science for ELLs

*Kristen Campbell Wilcox, University at Albany*

*Fang Yu, University at Albany*

The Next Generation Science Standards (NGSS; NGSS Lead States, 2013) emphasize that literacy skills are critical to building knowledge in science. These standards stress the importance of developing students' competencies in grasping the nature of evidence, attending to precision and detail in their explanations, making and assessing arguments, synthesizing complex information, and following detailed procedures and accounts of events (NGSS Lead States, 2013). These standards also correspond with the Common Core State Standards (CCSS) for literacy in history/social studies, science, and technical subjects that highlight developing discipline-specific reading and writing competencies in subject areas such as science (National Governors Association Center for Best Practices [NGA] & Council of Chief State School Officers [CCSSO], 2010a).

Given the demands of the CCSS, teachers are faced with a higher bar for rigor in how and what they teach with regard to reading and writing in their subject areas. The CCSS clearly present challenges not only for teachers in states where literacy standards for their subject areas were nonexistent or weak prior to the CCSS, but for students as well. These challenges can be even more acute for some ELLs who encounter challenges in subject-area classrooms such as science, as they may not have developed high levels of academic language competency before being mainstreamed and, once mainstreamed, not provided with sufficient scaffolding to assist them in navigating complex content and reading and writing tasks (Buxton & Lee, 2014; Lee, Quinn, & Valdés, 2013; Schmidt et al., 1997).

This chapter aims to provide a description of the CCSS content and linguistic demands for ELLs with a specific focus on writing, and provide some recommendations for writing instruction practice in secondary science classrooms based on prior research. We focus on writing as research has highlighted the strong correlations between writing and content learning, and the CCSS have reflected the importance of writing in content learning through the provision of writing standards in the content areas (Graham & Perin, 2007; Troia & Olinghouse, 2013). We begin with a summary of the content and linguistic demands of the CCSS and follow this with explanations and descriptions of recommended practices to address the content as well as linguistic demands ELLs face in secondary science classrooms.

## The Common Core State Standards and Specific Demands for ELLs

Through close examination of the CCSS for literacy in history/social studies, science, and technical subjects, we generated a list of key requirements for science writing within the four domains (text types and purposes, production and distribution of writing, research to build and present knowledge, and range of writing) highlighted in the CCSS (see Table 1). Although both science content learning and language learning demands increase as adolescents progress through secondary school, we summarized general features that are common across the grades here.

### Content Demands for CCSS-Aligned Instruction in Science

The CCSS call on science teachers to shift from traditional content learning approaches primarily dependent upon memorizing and reproducing information, often assessed through multiple choice and fill-in-the-blank exercises, to an emphasis on problem solving and critical thinking: These skills

### Table 1. Content and Linguistic Demands of the CSSS for Literacy in Science

| | Content Demands | Language Demands |
|---|---|---|
| Text Types and Purposes | • Introducing claims about topics or issues<br>• Supporting claims with reasoning and evidence | • Using words, phrases, and clauses to create cohesion<br>• Using appropriate structures in a discipline<br>• Using precise language and domain-specific vocabulary |
| Production and Distribution of Writing | | • Addressing specific purposes and audiences<br>• Using technology to share writing products |
| Research to Build and Present Knowledge | • Conducting research projects to answer questions or solve problems<br>• Gathering relevant information from multiple sources<br>• Drawing evidence to support analysis, reflection, and research | |
| Range of Writing | | • Writing routinely for a range of discipline-specific tasks, purposes, and audiences |

are more appropriately assessed through extended writing tasks of a paragraph or more that require interpretation of texts (Nachowitz, 2013; Olson et al., 2012). For example, in comparison to prior state standards and assessments, the CCSS place stronger emphasis on analysis (i.e., categorizing information, comparing and contrasting, and making inferences) than on procedural knowledge exhibited through such activities as following or outlining steps in a process (Porter, McMaken, Hwang, & Yang, 2011).

The benchmark writing samples provided in the CCSS reflect this emphasis on drawing evidence from texts and analyzing information (NGA & CCSSO, 2010b). These kinds of tasks are proposed as appropriate to prepare adolescents for success in postsecondary school science classrooms where they will be assigned a variety of extended writing tasks used to measure their content knowledge. These tasks range from simple summaries to complex arguments that require synthesis and analysis of large amounts of information from a variety of sources (Bunch, Kibler, & Pimentel, 2012). In addition, compared with prior state standards, the CCSS have increased the emphasis on solving what Porter and colleagues (2011) term "non-routine problems" (p. 109): Those problems that require students to apply and adapt a variety of problem-solving strategies in new ways.

Such emphases as discussed above demonstrate a relatively higher demand on adolescent learners than prior science standards, and they have been recommended by a number of scholars (Halliday & Martin, 1993; Hammond, 2001; Keys, 1999; Lee, Quinn, & Valdés; 2013; Lemke, 1990; O'Neill, 2001). While these increased demands on adolescent learners' expressions of content learning in and through writing seem to make sense and also are recommended in the research, they nonetheless can raise particularly daunting challenges to adolescent ELLs, as many of them are still developing the language competencies to access the meanings of the texts they read, and still developing their abilities to craft effective sentences using appropriate forms and academic vocabulary to express their understandings of those texts. In addition, they may not have been required to go beyond memorizing and reproducing information in mechanical tasks in science classrooms they attended in other countries (Buxton & Lee, 2014).

## Linguistic Demands for CCSS-Aligned Instruction in Science

The CCSS assume that all content teachers will assist students in developing competence in generic language conventions that provide cohesion (see Table 1). Likewise, the standards place the onus on science teachers to instruct students on how to successfully make the rhetorical moves characteristic of scientific argument such as stating claims, evidence, and warrants, all while using appropriate academic vocabulary.

The standards also recommend that students produce informative/explanatory and argument papers that are common in the discipline of science, and it is recommended that these writings be targeted to different disciplinary audiences. Research reports are an example of a typical and recommended writing task for secondary level science students. In the era of the CCSS, however, in order for research report tasks to meet the criteria of the CCSS, adolescents need to go beyond summarizing to synthesizing information gleaned through multiple sources, including those available on the Internet; introducing topics or issues of import in the discipline; supporting claims with source-based evidence; making arguments using sound reasoning and explanation; and, finally, providing conclusions drawn logically from information presented. When adolescents are producing such

CCSS-aligned written work in science classrooms, they are supposed to not only demonstrate their ability to communicate with accurate scientific vocabulary and conform to Standard English conventions, but also use language as a means to express their thinking in the unique ways scientists do. Keys (1999) described this kind of scientific literacy as including logical presentation, linear organization, and explicitness in connections between concepts.

In sum, the content and linguistic demands of the CCSS are inextricably linked to one another such that as adolescents engage in writing informative/explanatory and argument pieces that represent the "hidden rules" (Prain, 2006, p. 182) of the discipline of science, they are also simultaneously developing their understandings of scientific concepts, theories, and methodologies. Science educators, in the era of CCSS, are called upon to prepare their students to "learn language" and "learn though language" by engaging them in such disciplinary writing activities (Martin, 1993). Because the advanced disciplinary writing called for in the CCSS is one of the most challenging competencies ELLs develop, effective writing instruction must include careful scaffolding on the part of science teachers.

In the next section, we discuss some pedagogical recommendations to reach the goal of supporting ELLs' achievement in science, particularly through writing tasks, and follow this discussion with some examples from schools identified for exemplary writing instruction across the United States.

## Rationale

For ELLs to meet the CCSS for literacy in science, they need more than basic language proficiency, as discussed earlier; they need instruction in the unique features of science discourse encompassing scientific inquiry, explanation, and argumentation: the skills that are emphasized in both the CCSS and the NGSS.

Prior research has highlighted that ELLs face unique challenges in meeting the CCSS for literacy in science classrooms. First, as highlighted in both the National Assessment of Educational Progress report (National Assessment Governing Board, U.S. Department of Education, 2011) and studies on language minority students' science learning experiences (Duran, Dugan, & Weffer, 1998; Kearsey & Turner, 1999; Lee, 2005; Torres & Zeidler, 2002), ELLs may experience a mismatch between their prior linguistic and cultural experiences in science classrooms and the practices of Western science, such as conducting and reporting on research or engaging in argumentation around science topics. In addition, ELLs often arrive at school with different levels of basic interpersonal communication skills and cognitive academic language proficiencies (Cummins, 2008). Therefore, even those ELLs who have no difficulty in comprehending science content and expressing their understandings in everyday speech may still struggle to express their ideas in writing because of their perceived or real flawed academic written English competencies, which tend to mature later than other language competencies (Lee, Quinn, & Valdés, 2013).

With these challenges in mind, a few pedagogical practices are recommended for adolescent ELLs in science classrooms: the use of multimodal resources; problem-based learning activities; and explicit, individualized, and interactive instructional strategies.

## Multimodal Resources

Multimodal resources include those multimedia or digital texts that use images, words, sounds, or movement. The use of multimodal resources has been linked to various communicative functions important in conveying and perceiving science content such as gestures to convey movements/ changes or arrows to denote actions/sequences (Márquez, Izquierdo, & Espinet, 2006). As the CCSS requires students to engage with multimedia and digital texts, it is not sufficient for them to receive access to only those more traditional texts that explicate science vocabulary and content in textbooks. This is true for ELLs and non-ELLs alike. However, multimodal resources are highly recommended particularly for ELLs as these resources often help connect unfamiliar scientific concepts to everyday language and provide what many scholars have referred to as comprehensible input (Martin, 1993; Krashen, 1985; August & Shanahan, 2010).

## Problem-Based Learning Activities

Problem-based learning activities are those that engage learners in inquiry, and are sequential and collaborative. Features of problem-based activities include pursuing questions anchored in authentic or real-world problems; creating artifacts that apply concepts and represent knowledge of a problem; and collaborating with peers, teachers, and others in a disciplinary community with regard to a problem (Moje, Collazo, Carrillo, & Marx, 2001). These features respond to the content demands in the CCSS as students are engaged in identifying, investigating, and solving scientific problems and then presenting the results. Problem-based learning activities are particularly appropriate and useful for ELLs as they have opportunities to problematize subject matter and identify a variety of relevant resources to the problem at hand, and they are given time for sharing and revising their work and making sense with others (Engle & Conant, 2002).

## Explicit, Individualized, and Interactive Instructional Strategies

A long tradition of research has also pointed to the importance of balancing teacher-led explicit instruction with turn-taking that can take shape as dyadic (between two individuals such as a teacher and student or a student and student), but also triadic (between three individuals, or more—a teacher and students or a student and other students; Cumming, 2013). In addition to the importance of dyadic and triadic interactions for ELLs' sense-making, as the National Literacy Panel on Language Minority Children and Youth found (August & Shanahan, 2006), an important relationship exists between ELLs' development of oral and written proficiencies. Specifically, reading and writing proficiencies are highly correlated, and both are correlated with oral language proficiency (see Geva, 2006; Graham & Hebert, 2010). Therefore, classrooms in which ELLs are provided explicit instruction as well opportunities to engage in dyadic and triadic interactions are recommended (Lee, 2005; Snively & Corsiglia, 2001).

# Pedagogical Practice: Multimodal, Project-Based, and Interactive Instruction

We focus next on these three pedagogical practices found to be important in our own and others' research with regard to supporting ELLs' success in secondary science class work (Applebee & Langer, 2013; Wilcox, 2013; Wilcox, Yu, & Nachowitz, 2015). With a particular interest in the incorporation of writing in science classes, we found three common features of science classroom contexts where ELLs were successful in producing the kinds of writing that demonstrate meeting the CCSS for literacy in science. Because the use of multimodal resources, project-based writing activities, and explicit instruction balanced with dyadic and triadic interactional strategies can seem somewhat abstract, we offer here some examples of the practices and some artifacts that we identified in our study of schools with particularly effective instructional practices with regard to disciplinary writing.

## Portraits of Multimodal Instruction

The CCSS require students to write with discipline-specific language and vocabulary, as well as rhetorical structures characteristic of scientific discourse. Although it is challenging for many adolescents to do this, as writing in science is very different from other disciplinary writing, it can be particularly difficult for ELLs, some of whom may still be developing basic language proficiencies. However, teachers' use of multimodal resources can be helpful as they may facilitate alternate pathways to comprehend and express understandings of science content.

What does the use of multimodal resources in instruction look like in the secondary science classroom? In our study, ELLs in the more successful classrooms were exposed to linguistic resources in the form of text as well as other symbolic representations like drawings, diagrams, songs, and videos. For example, one 12th-grade biology teacher invited students to alter popular song lyrics and replace them with biology terms; in a sixth-grade earth science classroom, students were instructed to watch a video on rock formations and then craft a representation of what they learned in a diagram (see Figure 1). In this sixth-grade classroom, the science teacher reminded students of the information from the video and encouraged them to connect what they watched to what they wrote. As can be seen in the writing sample in Figure 1, while few words are used, the student successfully expressed his content knowledge by relating complex science concepts to one another.

In another example, a 10th-grade physics teacher worked with students in a science lab explaining how a pendulum worked and how to measure time based on the swings of a pendulum. The teacher started the lesson by making a real pendulum and showing it to students without explaining the mechanics. He tied a weight to the end of a thin 5-ft rope that was attached to the ceiling. He held the weight shoulder height and 3 to 4 ft away from the center point, and then released the weight so that it swung away from him and back toward him to show how a pendulum worked. When demonstrating it, the teacher introduced the word "pendulum" by sharing one of Edgar Allen Poe's stories: "The Pit and the Pendulum." Afterward, students received a handout of related concepts and vocabulary. The teacher instructed students to read the handouts, and then posted questions about how people in the past told time. After a brief discussion on Galileo's use of astronomy to determine time, he created a game for students in which they would measure pendulum swings by noting how much time there was between the start and end of a swing. Then, students were instructed to describe in writing what a pendulum was in their own words without worrying about using "science language." Students were allowed to draw their understandings (as in the Figure 1 example) if they chose, instead of expressing their understandings in narrative form.

This example demonstrates how a science teacher used multimodal resources to engage students in using science language to convey content knowledge. The teacher applied an experiment to

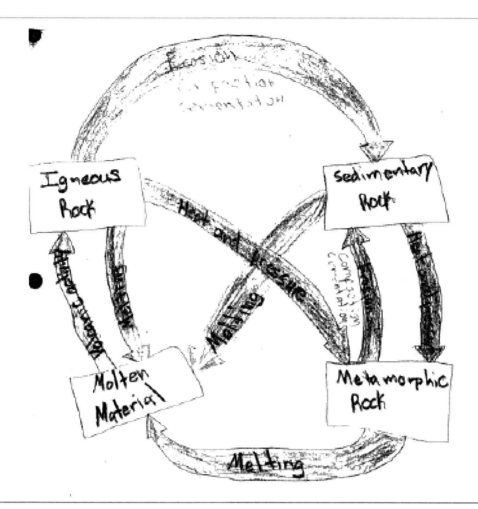

*Figure 1. A Student's Writing Product on Rock Formations*

offer students a direct and intuitive impression of what a pendulum was and how it worked. He also engaged students with appealing stories ("The Pit and the Pendulum" and Galileo's story), creatively connecting science content with literature and real life scenarios. The handout served as another resource of language and content input, which students could refer to when participating in the game and writing up or drawing the results. The science teacher's use of multimodal resources enriched the original concept of the pendulum. Students had the opportunity to access the concept in a variety of ways including through experimentation, evoking real life scenarios, and through literature.

We also identified science teachers placing an emphasis on the use of technology as a multimodal resource. Both students and science teachers reported that they often used the Internet to research information or simulate natural phenomena. Teachers also encouraged students to read research articles from the Internet and write reflections on what they read digitally. In this way, students were not constrained to static "knowledge-out-of-context" from their textbooks, but had the opportunity to be exposed to dynamic "knowledge-in-action" available through technology (Applebee, 1996, p. 1).

In sum, these uses of multimodal resources in science classrooms resonate with findings of some scholars that note the importance of connecting emerging science content knowledge and academic vocabulary to students' past experiences and everyday language (Hand, Lawrence, & Yore, 2010; Lemke, 1990; Prain, 2006). As the development of domain-specific vocabulary is a focus in the CCSS, it is important for teachers to teach it in a way that connects to ELLs' linguistic resources from prior experiences (Moll, Amanti, Neff, & Gonzalez, 1992), and, thereby, makes the process of learning new vocabulary and the understandings of relationships between complex concepts accessible.

## What a Science Teacher Can Do

Given that the integration of multimodal resources is associated with better learning outcomes for ELLs, science teachers should encourage an abundance of dyadic and triadic talk, symbolic as well as narrative writing, and opportunities for extralinguistic (e.g., gesture) expression to facilitate learning. In planning, teachers can consider:

a. Emphasizing the use of visuals, such as pictures, figures, graphs, charts, tables, and so on, as visual representations offer ELLs alternative means to access content which may otherwise be too complicated for them to understand, if delivered only orally or in text.

b. Developing alternative criteria to assess content knowledge such as providing the option for symbolic writing (as in the example in Figure 1).

c. Allowing ELLs to use nonstandard forms or informal English to express their ideas, focusing on the substance of their ideas rather than on producing "error-free writing in terms of syntax, conventions and mechanics," which can disrupt sense-making (Wilcox & Jeffery, 2015, p. 54).

d. Integrating technologies in purposeful ways that facilitate comprehension and production of texts (iPads, Chromebooks, Internet, etc.).

## Portraits of Project-Based Writing Activities

We also identified that science teachers in schools with exemplary outcomes for ELLs in terms of their written work assigned project-based activities rather than "one-and-done" writing assignments. Before producing a final writing product, students were engaged in a series of process-writing activities recommended in the research (Silva, 2008) including teacher-guided discussions, brainstorming, reading topic-related articles, and writing multiple drafts. Students also had the opportunity to review their peers' essays and then revise their own writing based on their peers' and teachers' feedback. They were often required to present their final writing products supplemented by multimedia presentations, such as in PowerPoint, as well. These kinds of project-based writing assignments create meaningful opportunities for ELLs to communicate understandings of disciplinary texts and content and are preferable to mechanical tasks such as multiple-choice and fill-in-the-blank exercises, which do not meet the CCSS for literacy in science well (Bunch, Lotan, Valdés, & Cohen, 2005; Valdés, 2001).

In one example of the use of such project-based learning strategies, in a biology class observed as part of our study, students took turns reading handouts aloud and then responded to short-answer questions on their worksheets. However, the lesson did not stop there. The teacher directed students to later use their worksheet answers as a source of reference for an extended writing task as part of a project. When students finished their writing, the science teacher discussed and reviewed their written work with the whole class and critically pointed out the places that needed to be improved both in terms of language and content. In this way, students were given explicit feedback on both the quality of the writing itself as well as on the content expressed in the writing.

In some cases, science teachers in our study not only implemented project-based writing assignments in their own classes, but also collaborated with teachers in other content classrooms to engage students in interdisciplinary writing projects. For example, a biology teacher in our study collaborated with a same-grade level English language arts (ELA) teacher guiding students to read the book *Life of Pi* (Yann Martel, 2001, Random House of Canada) and write reflections on the science content illustrated in the book. The science teacher noted that the book was perfect for such an interdisciplinary project because "it contained a lot of science knowledge like animal behavior and brain physiology" (personal communication, April, 28, 2009). In this semester-long project, students were required to engage in a range of tasks that included reading the book with the guidance of both the science and ELA teachers, selecting relevant quotes, analyzing scientific content in the book, and producing reading reflection papers.

Our last example of a project-based writing assignment was in sixth-grade ELL Julio's classroom. In our interview with Julio, he reported that while a rainforest project was "time-consuming and required a lot of work" in which he had to "write a ton of notes" (personal communication, 2009) he learned about important concepts such as deforestation, regeneration, and habitat. Julio explained that he was instructed to choose a forest animal from the list provided by his teacher and to seek further information on this animal from "books and the Internet and anything we could find research about it" (personal communication, 2009). When Julio had sufficient background information from a variety of texts, he was guided by his teacher to write a research report that included a statement of a hypothesis, evidence, findings, and a conclusion. Finally, he was encouraged to use Windows Media or PowerPoint to share his research findings with his class.

This rainforest project resulted in not only a written product, but a process of doing scientific research in ways that build scientific literacies (Hand, 1999; Keys, 1999; Lee, 2005; Lemke, 1990; MacArthur, Graham, & Fitzgerald, 2008; Moje, Collazo, Carrillo, & Marx, 2001; Prain, 2006; Quinn, Lee, & Valdés, 2012). Although Julio perceived this project as challenging, he received a great deal of support from his teachers and multiple sources of linguistic input (e.g. notes, handouts, books, multimedia on the Internet). This project demonstrates a successful scenario of how teachers used a project-based writing activity to help a sixth-grade ELL to understand science content and develop complex scientific knowledge as well as oral and written competencies (Shein, 2012).

Project-based pedagogy has been recommended in the research literature (Buxton & Lee, 2014; Moje, Collazo, Carrillo, & Marx, 2001; Quinn, Lee, & Valdés, 2012) in order to engage ELLs in authentic science learning experiences which offer them an opportunity to inquire and explore questions of interest. When preparing a project-based lesson for ELLs, teachers may consider the following:

a. Offering ELLs a variety of reading materials (e.g., articles, handouts, novels) that express content in different ways

b. Engaging ELLs in a series of process-writing activities including brainstorming, writing reflections on topic-related texts, and crafting multiple drafts

c. Providing opportunities for ELLs to discuss projects with their peers, to review their peers' writing, and to revise their own writing based on their peers' and teachers' feedback

d. Allowing ELLs to present their final writing products supplemented by multimedia presentations instead of solely writing texts

e. Collaborating with teachers in other disciplines (e.g., ELA or ESL teachers) to engage ELLs in interdisciplinary writing activities

## Portraits of Explicit, Individualized, and Interactive Writing Instruction

In addition to the benefits of using multimodal resources and engaging ELLs in project-based writing activities, a combination of explicit teaching and interactive instructional practices were offered to ELLs in the more effective schools we studied. We noted science teachers in these schools tended to explicitly direct students in how to set goals and timelines for writing and provided supplemental resources (e.g., lists of science terminology) that students could refer to when completing their writing tasks. These teachers also explicitly taught students foundational writing skills (e.g., how to organize ideas in paragraphs and how to proofread their own as well as their peers' writing). In addition, they provided text-structure instruction (e.g., how to construct a hypothesis and conclusion as part of a research report assignment) and gave critical feedback to point out strengths and weaknesses in students' writing. This process of teachers' involvement in providing explicit writing instruction in science classrooms represents an apprenticeship learning model in which novice learners observe, imitate, and practice in supervised participation in writing activities and is recommended in the CCSS (Kibler, Walqui, & Bunch, 2014; Rogoff, 1990).

Teachers in the schools also expressed awareness of ELLs' various levels of language proficiency and attempted to individualize their instruction to meet their needs. For example, Julio, introduced earlier, regularly participated in an after-school program which offered him individual tutorials in science. This type of individualized instruction was also identified at other schools in our study as teachers from different disciplines rotated to help ELLs with their subject-area work after school on a daily basis. In alignment with this individualized approached to ELLs' needs, in some of the science classes we observed, teachers purposely set up different learning goals for ELLs and non-ELLs, and took into account students' proficiencies when selecting texts.

In the classrooms we observed, dyadic and triadic interactions were emphasized as well. Students were encouraged to negotiate understandings of science content with their peers and prompted to challenge each other's solutions to problems. A substantial amount of pair and group work was observed in which students brainstormed on topics and issues, shared writing, and provided peer feedback. The science department chair in one school expressed the importance of such ELL and non-ELL peer interactions: "The kids are grouped by being totally blended. I think it helps kids that are struggling. They get to see how other kids are doing it; they see role models" (personal communication, April 27, 2009).

Teachers' instructions play an important role in ELLs' scientific content learning and disciplinary writing development. Science teachers may consider

a. explicitly modeling the procedure to complete a writing task from setting goals and managing timelines to proofreading drafts before final submission.

b. providing text-structure instruction (e.g., how to construct a hypothesis and conclusion statement as part of a research report assignment) and writing samples to ELLs.

c. differentiating instruction and designing different goals for writing products for ELLs and non-ELLs.

d. providing ELLs individual and specific feedback on their writing in or after class. One-one tutoring time with ELLs after school is also recommended.

In this section, we described three pedagogical recommendations for ELLs to meet the CCSS in secondary science classrooms: the use of multimodal resources; problem-based writing activities; and explicit, individualized, and interactive instructional strategies. While these recommendations are research supported and intuitively appealing, they are also not simple for secondary school science teachers to implement. Reaching the vision of the CCSS in science is also not simple for ELLs. The content and linguistic demands of secondary science are formidable, yet with multi-modal resources and project-based writing activities supported through explicit writing instruction that is both individualized and interactive, ELLs in our studies achieved quite high levels of writing proficiency (Wilcox, Yu, & Nachowitz, 2015) and exhibited high levels of content knowledge.

Ultimately, the task of preparing ELLs to meet the CCSS in science is best tackled through a collaborative approach. Therefore, in the next section, we provide some ideas for reflection and discussion you may find useful to guide your collaborations with other teachers in your school or district.

## Reflection Questions and Action Plans

1. Looking back at the sections on portraits of multimodal resources, project-based writing, and explicit, individualized, and interactive instruction, what are some of the ways you might incorporate these resources and strategies in your instruction?

   a. With colleagues, identify your ELLs' listening, speaking, reading, and writing needs. For example, do they need more multimodal resources and activities to enhance their comprehension of texts, or more practice with writing summaries or arguments? What resources do you already have available to attend to these needs? And for those resources you do not have, consider how might you attain and integrate them in your instruction.

   b. Develop a chart that you can use as a reminder about particular multimodal resources, project-based activities, and interactive classroom strategies you can use in your unit and lesson plans to address your ELLs' needs.

c. Brainstorm specific reading and writing activities that provide opportunities for your ELLs to comprehend and express their content knowledge in various ways such as through song, diagram, video, and so on.

2. What are some of the big ideas or major concepts you want ELLs to learn from your lessons this year? Invite colleagues in your subject area to choose one big idea and plan specific project-based writing activities around it to make it accessible to ELLs.

   a. Integrate a range of problem-solving, hands-on, and inquiry-based activities that invite frequent opportunities for ELLs to speak and write about these big ideas throughout the year.

   b. Use the writing activities to help students explore the concepts, make connections, extend connections, and generate new connections to the content and to their own lives. Because one focus of these tasks is on the content, allow for the use of native language or other symbolic forms of writing (e.g., tables or charts, numbers, figures) when they are composing. Provide models for all writing tasks.

3. What are some of the writing skills you would like to see developed among the ELLs in your classroom this year? Invite colleagues from other subject areas to discuss interdisciplinary projects that might incorporate developing these skills.

   a. Develop a chart that outlines the writing skills each subject area specialist sees as important for ELLs' success in their respective classes. From this chart, consider what skills will be developed in which classes and as part of what units of instruction throughout the school year. Crosswalk these with Table 1 and other CCSS materials to ensure CCSS alignment.

4. With your colleagues, develop rubrics for students and teachers to use in evaluating writing. Consider: What characteristics of writing are important in our discipline?

   a. Include separate sections for content, organization, language, and conventions so that surface-level errors such as spelling or capitalization do not dominate the feedback students receive on their writing. Rather, ensure that the ideas expressed in the writing are acknowledged and celebrated.

   b. Collect a set of writing samples for students to analyze that highlight the features of more and less successful writing of various types required in your science classrooms.

   c. Instruct students to use rubrics to evaluate their own writing as well as their peers' writing before submitting their final writing products. Direct them to revise and resubmit their writing based on your feedback and their peers' comments.

5. Discuss with your students how they can present and share their final writing products using multimedia (e.g., Windows Media, PowerPoint, Prezi).

   a. Integrate technology in your regular class work, particularly in ways where students have hands-on access directly to technology.

b. Instruct students to work in groups on multimedia presentations and publications of their writing products using different technologies and targeted to different audiences.

c. Instruct students to provide feedback on their peers' multimedia presentations or publications using rubrics.

# References

Applebee, A. N. (1996). *Curriculum as conversation: Transforming traditions of teaching and learning.* Chicago, IL: University of Chicago Press.

Applebee, A. N., & Langer, J. A. (2013). *Writing instruction that works: Proven methods for middle and high school classrooms.* New York, NY: Teachers College Press.

August, D., & Shanahan, T. (Eds.). (2006). *Developing literacy in second-language learners: Report of the National Literacy Panel on Language-Minority Children and Youth.* Mahwah, NJ: Lawrence Erlbaum Associates.

August, D., & Shanahan, T. (2010). Effective English literacy instruction for English learners. In California Department of Education (Ed.), *Improving education for English learners: Research-based approaches.* Sacramento, CA: California Department of Education Press.

Bunch, G., Kibler, A., & Pimentel, S. (2012). *Realizing opportunities for English learners in the Common Core English language arts and disciplinary literacy standards.* Stanford, CA: Understanding Language Initiative.

Bunch, G., Lotan, R., Valdés, G., & Cohen, E. (2005). Keeping content at the heart of content-based instruction: Access and support for transitional English learners. In J. Crandall & D. Kaufman (Eds.), *Content-based instruction in primary and secondary school settings* (pp. 11–25). Alexandria, VA: Teachers of English to Speakers of Other Languages.

Buxton, C. A., & Lee, O. (2014). English language learners in science education. In N. G. Lederman & S. K. Abell (Eds.), *Handbook of research in science education* (2nd ed., pp. 204–222). Mahwah, NJ: Lawrence Erlbaum Associates.

Cumming, A. (2013). Multiple dimensions of academic language and literacy development. *Language Learning, 63*(1), 130–152.

Cummins, J. (2008). BICS and CALP: Empirical and theoretical status of the distinction. In B. Street & N. H. Hornberger (Eds.), *Encyclopedia of language and education* (pp. 487–499). New York, NY: Springer US.

Duran, B. J., Dugan, T., & Weffer, R. (1998). Language minority students in high school: The role of language in learning biology concepts. *Science Education, 82*(3), 311–341.

Engle, R. A., & Conant, F. R. (2002). Guiding principles for fostering productive disciplinary engagement: Explaining an emergent argument in a community of learners classroom. *Cognition and Instruction, 20*(4), 399–483.

Geva, E. (2006). Second-language oral proficiency and second-language literacy. In D. August & T. Shanahan (Eds.), *Developing literacy in second-language learners: Report of the National Literacy Panel on Language-Minority Children and Youth.* Mahwah, NJ: Lawrence Erlbaum Associates.

Graham, S., & Hebert, M. (2010). *Writing to read: Evidence for how writing can improve reading. Carnegie Corporation time to act report.* Washington, DC: Alliance for Excellent Education.

Graham, S., & Perin, D. (2007). *Writing next: Effective strategies to improve writing of adolescents in middle and high school.* Washington, DC: Alliance for Excellence in Education.

Halliday, M., & Martin, J. (1993). *Writing science: Literacy and discursive power.* London, England: Falmer Press.

Hammond, L. (2001). Notes from California: An anthropological approach to urban science education for language minority families. *Journal of Research in Science Teaching, 38*(9), 983–999.

Hand, B., Lawrence, C., & Yore, L. D. (1999). A writing in science framework designed to enhance science literacy. *International Journal of Science Education, 21*(10), 1021–1035.

Kearsey, J., & Turner, S. (1999). The value of bilingualism in pupils' understanding of scientific language. *International Journal of Science Education, 21*(10), 1037–1050.

Keys, C. W. (1999). Revitalizing instruction in scientific genres: Connecting knowledge production with writing to learn in science. *Science Education, 83*(2), 115–130.

Kibler, A. K., Walqui, A., & Bunch, G. C. (2014). Transformational opportunities: Language and literacy instruction for English language learners in the Common Core era in the United States. *TESOL Journal, 6,* 9–35.

Krashen, S. D. (1985). *The input hypothesis: Issues and implications.* London, England: Longman.

Lee, O. (2005). Science education with English language learners: Synthesis and research agenda. *Review of Educational Research, 75*(4), 491–530.

Lee, O., Quinn, H., & Valdés, G. (2013). Science and language for English language learners in relation to Next Generation Science Standards and with implications for Common Core State Standards for English language arts and mathematics. *Educational Researcher, 42*(4), 223–233.

Lemke, J. L. (1990). *Talking science: Language, learning, and values.* Norwood, NJ: Ablex.

MacArthur, C. A., Graham, S., & Fitzgerald, J. (Eds.). (2008). *Handbook of writing research.* New York, NY: Guilford Press.

Márquez, C., Izquierdo, M., & Espinet, M. (2006). Multimodal science teachers' discourse in modeling the water cycle. *Science Education, 90*(2), 202–226.

Martin, J. (1993). Mentoring semiogenesis: "genre-based" literacy pedagogy. In F. Christie (Ed.), *Pedagogy and the shaping of consciousness: Linguistic and social processes* (pp. 123–155). London, England: Cassell.

Moje, E. B., Collazo, T., Carrillo, R., & Marx, R. W. (2001). "Maestro, what is 'quality'?": Language, literacy, and discourse in project-based science. *Journal of Research in Science Teaching, 38*(4), 469–498.

Moll, L. C., Amanti, C., Neff, D., & Gonzalez, N. (1992). Funds of knowledge for teaching: Using a qualitative approach to connect homes and classrooms. *Theory into Practice, 31*(2), 132–141.

Nachowitz, M. (2013).Writing in science. In A. N. Applebee & J. A. Langer (Eds.), *Writing instruction that works: Proven methods for middle and high school classrooms* (pp. 94–110). New York, NY: Teachers College Press.

National Assessment Governing Board, U.S. Department of Education (2011). *Science Framework for the 2011 National Assessment of Educational Progress.* Retrieved from http://www.nagb.org/publications /frameworks/science/2011-science-framework.html

National Governors Association Center for Best Practices & Council of Chief State School Officers. (2010a). *Common Core State Standards for English language arts and literacy in history/social studies, science, and technical subjects.* Washington, DC: Authors. Retrieved from www.corestandards.org/assets/CCSSI _ELA%20Standards.pdf

National Governors Association Center for Best Practices & Council of Chief State School Officers. (2010b). *Common Core State Standards for English language arts & literacy in history/social studies, science, and technical subjects: Appendix C: Samples of student writing.* Washington, DC: Authors. Retrieved from http:// www.corestandards.org/assets/Appendix_C.pdf

NGSS Lead States. (2013). *Next Generation Science Standards: For states, by states.* Washington, DC: National Academies Press.

Olson, C. B., Kim, J. S., Scarcella, R., Kramer, J., Pearson, M., van Dyk, D. A., Collins, P., & Land, R. E. (2012). Enhancing the interpretive reading and analytical writing of mainstreamed English learners in secondary school. *American Educational Research Journal, 49*(2), 323–355.

O'Neill, D. K. (2001). Knowing when you've brought them in: Scientific genre knowledge and communities of practice. *The Journal of the Learning Sciences, 10*(3), 223–264.

Porter, A., McMaken, J., Hwang, J., & Yang, R. (2011). Common Core Standards: The new U.S. intended curriculum. *Educational researcher, 40*(3), 103–116.

Prain, V. (2006). Learning from writing in secondary science: Some theoretical and practical implications. *International Journal of Science Education, 28*(2–3), 179–201.

Quinn, H., Lee, O., & Valdés, G. (2012). *Language demands and opportunities in relation to Next Generation Science Standards for English language learners: What teachers need to know.* Stanford, CA: Understanding Language Initiative.

Rogoff, B. (1990). *Apprenticeship in thinking: Cognitive development in social context.* New York, NY: Oxford University Press.

Schmidt, W. H., McKnight, C. C., Raizen, S. A., Jakwerth, P. M., Valverde, G. A., Wolfe, R. G., & Houang, R. T. (1997). *A splintered vision: An investigation of U.S. science and mathematics education* (Vol. 3). Boston, MA: Kluwer Academic.

Shein, P. P. (2012). Seeing with two eyes: A teacher's use of gestures in questioning and revoicing to engage English language learners in the repair of mathematical errors. *Journal for Research in Mathematics Education, 43*(2), 182–222.

Silva, T. (2008). *A synthesis of the results of basic research on second language writing: 1980 to 2005.* Paper presented at the Writing Research Across Borders Conference, Santa Barbara, CA.

Snively, G., & Corsiglia, J. (2001). Discovering indigenous science: Implications for science education. *Science Education, 85*(1), 6–34.

Torres, H. N., & Zeidler, D. L. (2002). The effects of English language proficiency and scientific reasoning skills on the acquisition of science content knowledge by Hispanic English language learners and native English language speaking students. *Electronic Journal of Science Education, 6*(3). Retrieved from http://ejse.southwestern.edu/article/view/7683/5450

Troia, G. A., & Olinghouse, N. G. (2013). The Common Core State Standards and evidence-based educational practices: The case of writing. *School Psychology Review, 42*(3), 343–357.

Valdés, G. (2001). *Learning and not learning English: Latino students in American schools. Multicultural Education Series.* New York, NY: Teachers College Press.

Wilcox, K. C. (2013). Writing instruction for English language learners. In A. N. Applebee & J. A. Langer (Eds.), *Writing instruction that works: Proven methods for middle and high school classrooms* (pp. 130–144). New York, NY: Teachers College Press.

Wilcox, K. C., & Jeffery, J. V. (2015). Adolescent English language learners' stances toward disciplinary writing. *English for Specific Purposes, 38,* 44–56.

Wilcox, K. C., Yu, F., & Nachowitz, M. (2015). Epistemic complexity in adolescent writing. *Journal of Writing Research, 7*(1), 5–39.

# Guided Visualization: Promoting ELL Science Literacies Through Images

*Alandeom W. Oliveira, State University of New York at Albany*

*Molly H. Weinburgh, Texas Christian University*

The introduction of two important documents has influenced how science educators and science teachers think about science, language, and the intersection of those two disciplines. Of direct importance to science teachers are the Next Generation Science Standards (NGSS; NGSS Lead States, 2013), which were developed to be guideposts for district and state personnel responsible for curriculum and to provide a structure for discussing the integration across the disciplines of science, mathematics, technology, and English. These science standards outline disciplinary content ideas, cross-cutting concepts, and science practices to be mastered as students move through K–12 education. Of interest is the way the NGSS have forefronted and stressed communication as one of the practices of science.

The second document, although preceding the NGSS, has less direct influence on science teaching but has the potential to provide guidance for science teachers and researchers. The Common Core State Standards (CCSS; National Governors Association Center for Best Practices [NGA] & Council of Chief State School Officers [CCSSO], 2010) stress communication skills and call upon student engagement in visual communication as a means to develop science literacy. As evident in the recurrent allusions to nonverbal forms of representation prevalent in scientific texts (graphs, diagrams, and tables) in these standards, visual production and reception constitute important components of the set of reading, writing, speaking, and listening abilities that students are expected to develop as a result of their participation in science instruction. To be considered scientifically literate, students need to be able to transform texts into visuals (plot or diagram textually encoded content) as well as convert visuals into texts (verbally decode visual representations). Put differently, students need to be able to produce, interpret, and transpose scientific information across visual and textual formats.

These visual demands of the CCSS create new opportunities and challenges for ELLs faced with the complex task of having to learn science in a new language. On the one hand, it creates educational opportunities in the form of added impetus to make science instruction more visual, and hence more accessible to nonnative speakers of English. On the other hand, more heavily embracing the visual mode of communication in science inevitably means that more careful and critical consideration should be given by instructors for visual literacy and its potential impact on student conceptual mastery and language acquisition.

## The Common Core State Standards and Specific Demands for ELLs

Our pedagogical practice addresses the CCSS standards of reading and writing for English language arts (ELA) and for literacy in science (NGA & CCSSO, 2010). The subcategory of "Integration of Knowledge and Ideas" begins in kindergarten with students being able to "describe the relationship between illustrations and the text" (RI.K.7; p. 13). The student requirements increase each year so that by the 12th grade, students should be able to "integrate and evaluate multiple sources of information presented in different media or formats (e.g., visually, quantitatively) as well as in words in order to address a question or solve a problem" (RI.11–12.7; p. 40) as an ELA requirement. In addition, the literacy in science standards specifically indicate that the text is "scientific" and "technical" rather than narrative (NGA & CCSSO, 2010, pp. 13–14).

At first glance, this may seem to be a straightforward task of pointing out pictures and graphs or asking students to draw what they see. However, in addition to the general difficulty of interpretation (Ametller & Pinto, 2002), research shows that visual communication is culturally specific rather than universal; the imagery used for communication is reflective of existing visual cultures (Sturken & Cartwright, 2009). Members of particular cultural groups have preferred ways of seeing or looking that may differ from other groups. Their visual representations of the world (for example, drawings and paintings) are cultural manifestations of larger societal developments and carry unique cultural meanings. Likewise, science itself has its unique visual culture characterized by highly specialized forms of visual representation (abstract images designed according to scientific visual conventions, symbolism, and notation). This is in sharp contrast to lay visual communication, which favors everyday/realistic imagery devoid of specialized language (Kress & van Leeuwen, 2006). Therefore, cultural differences and lack of familiarity with scientific visuals can hinder rather than facilitate the learning of science content by ELLs. In an effort to prevent such complications, this chapter focuses on the practice of "guided visualization," image-centered pedagogical strategies used by science teachers to help ELLs cope with the visual demands of the CCSS.

## Rationale

The latter part of the 20th century introduced an important paradigm shift in science education as more researchers began investigating the role of language in science and science education (Lehesvuori, Viiri, Rasku-Puttonem, Moate, & Helaakoski, 2013; Lemke, 1998, 2004; Roth, 2004, 2008,

2014; Yore, 2004). This shift theorizes language (the human capability to acquire and use intricate systems of communication) as both the tool and medium for learning, allowing human beings to converse both verbally and nonverbally with an audience. Of particular note is the notion of the hybrid nature of science language (Lemke, 1998, 2004). This hybrid language consists of natural language (for us, this is English), mathematical expressions, visual representations, and meaningful, specialized actions within the situational contexts of science. This more broadly conceived idea of literacies embeds the various modalities within unique contexts (Gee, 2004; Lave & Wenger, 1991) as ways in which those belonging to a community are able to communicate.

Science as an enterprise must use communication modalities that go beyond natural language (Lemke, 2004), requiring students to integrate different media and formats as part of textual material. Visual representations as a meaning-making and meaning-communication tool can extend and enhance natural language. The importance of this modality for students is becoming more evident to science teachers. In addition, the growing evidence of the role that different cultural backgrounds play in how students present and interpret visuals highlights the need to give particular attention to visuals when working with ELLs.

Science teachers need to first become aware of the unique perspectives that ELLs may bring to the science text and, then, to practice pedagogies that can help students develop the ability to express thoughts and concepts as visuals as well as interpret the visuals that are found in texts. Students from different cultural and linguistic backgrounds bring a wealth of experiences and ideas to the U.S. classroom. For students who have not mastered the use of English, visual forms of communication can allow them to demonstrate content knowledge while developing language skills.

Science educators have become increasingly aware of the need to support student development of visual literacy (that is, the ability to critically interpret images) in science. While evidence exists that visuals can indeed foster student learning of science content (Ainsworth, Prain, & Tytler, 2011; Gilbert, Reiner, & Nakhleh, 2008), research also shows that secondary students often have difficulty in interpreting illustrations in science textbooks (Ametller & Pinto, 2002; Catley, Novick, & Shade, 2010). An inability to interpret visuals can lead to science learning problems as well as poor academic performance. Therefore, teachers should not simply assume that science images are self-evident (transparent) to students. Further, helping students overcome eventual difficulties requires explicit instruction in how to "read" specific types of visuals. Vasquez, Comer, and Troutman (2010) recommend that teachers explicitly comment on illustrative techniques, discuss the visual features of analytical diagrams, highlight key visual attributes of images, and help students scan and navigate illustrations.

In this chapter, we discuss the content and linguistic demands that ELLs face in secondary science classes whose teachers have embraced visualization as outlined in the CCSS Reading Standards for Literacy in Science and Technical Subjects 6–12. These standards require students to accurately decipher and decode science texts and to produce all the "diverse formats and media" (RST.11–12.7; p. 62) found in scientific writing. We give attention specifically to pedagogical strategies adopted by two high-school science teachers in New York state to help students translate, decode, and encode natural language and visual representation. Both teachers were experienced, had received professional development such as SIOP training, and were in the process of aligning their classroom practices with CCSS for science and technical subjects. Collectively named "guided visualization," these visual pedagogies are used to help ELLs become more fluent in multiple literacies of science.

## Pedagogical Practice: Guided Visualization

Guided visualization refers to science teaching approaches centered on imagery (photos, diagrams, and graphs). Acting as a guide, the teacher facilitates interactive classroom activities such as whole-class discussion and small-group work that involve pictorial representations—two-dimensional visual depictions, such as images, diagrams, and graphs, of natural phenomena. The teacher prompts articulation of prior understandings, provides feedback and guidance, and supports students (both conceptually and linguistically) as they collaboratively construct word-image relations of meaning.

The practice of guided visualization is characterized by two main pedagogical features: shared visual focus and dialogue. Teachers and students have a shared visual landscape (a collective focus of reference for interactions) that provides them with a cognitive space for joint interpretive work such as making sense of natural phenomena and thinking through problems together. Further, guided visualization resembles a dialogue in the sense that students' ideas and views are listened to and taken into account by teachers and peers. Rather than being limited to expository transmission or direct instruction, teachers and students also engage in exploratory and responsive discussion wherein participants collaboratively build on each other's ideas. The two main formats or variations of guided visualization—visual decoding and visual encoding—are described below.

### Visual Decoding

Visual decoding fundamentally involves teacher-guided interpretation of scientific imagery, such as a diagram of a cell cycle. Typically, this takes the form of writing assignments or discussion activities in which visually encoded science content is collaboratively expressed in words by teachers and students. Visual representations are collectively verbalized under the guidance of a science teacher. This particular form of guided visualization was used by Mary, a 10th-grade biology teacher, during a lesson on human reproduction. With 9 ELLs in a class of 28 students, Mary set out to teach the anatomy and physiology of female reproductive structures involved in human fetal development. To do so, she utilized a PowerPoint slideshow with a series of highly realistic photographs of a dissection that she had previously performed on a pregnant bovine uterus donated to her by the agricultural program of a local university. Drawing on the high degree of similarity between bovine and human reproductive organs, Mary encouraged students to see what a real reproduction system looks like during the process of gestation. In Mary's own words, "I tried to make the input flood of content vocabulary more comprehensible by contextualizing it with visuals that were virtual and physical and oral, and written language was consistently linked with both [sic], and to provide another opportunity for students to hear and see key vocabulary." Student expressions of disgust and discomfort (giggles) could be heard in the background in response to the bloody and slimy images. (See Figure 1.)

Particularly noticeable in Mary's approach to guided visualization is her strong focus on scientific nomenclature. Throughout the discussion, she prioritizes naming the different parts of a cow's

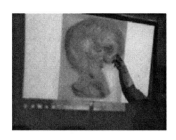

Mary: So this is the uterus here, there's no baby in this side but there is a baby in this side. And here is an ovary, and this is part of the cervix and the vagina. Alright? And in the cow the vagina can be very long, like as long as somebody's arm because it's a very big animal.

Mary: Now, I took a knife, a scalpel, and I cut open the wall of the ovary, of the uterus, and this is the amniotic sac. The bag, the amniotic sac [holds up a transparent plastic bag with a doll inside] so it would be the baby inside here . . . So this bag is full of liquid, amniotic fluid. And that is what [points back to screen] this is. And this is the uterus wall around it.

Student: What are these little patches on there?

Mary: That's a good question. These are the types of placentas that a cow has, a very different kind of placenta. We humans have a big placenta, one big placenta but cows have these little tiny placentas. This is the mother's side of the placenta and this is the baby's side of the placenta, and they're together and exchange liquids between.

Mary: There's the baby, this is the amniotic fluid, now it looks like it has much more blood than it really does. It's mostly clear liquid, a little bit yellowish, but because there's a little bit of blood mixed in with it it looks like there's much blood. And this is what comes out when a woman is pregnant and she's going into labor and the uterus starts to push the baby, and then this bag opens. And sometimes it happens when the woman is in the grocery store or in the car, or at home, you don't know when it's going to happen.

Mary: What's this part right here?

Student: Umbilical cord.

Mary: Umbilical cord, very good, and it's connected somewhere down to here to the placenta. Alright, so there's the umbilical cord more close, and you can see blood vessels, arteries and veins, and then down here somewhere it's connected to the placenta.

*Figure 1. Mary's Presentation and Discussion*

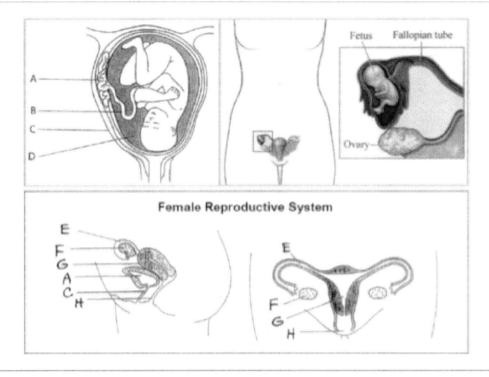

*Figure 2. Diagrammatic Representations of the Female Human Reproduction System*

reproductive system portrayed in each photograph: ovary, cervix, vagina, uterus, amniotic sac, placenta, umbilical cord, blood vessels, arteries, and veins. By doing so, she helps students visually decode (read) the biological images. Mary provides students with guidance on how to "translate" the photographic contents into words that are consistent with professional jargon (standard scientific terminology). Students are shown how to verbalize visual representations of an organism's biological entrails.

To help her ELLs cope with content and language demands of biology instruction, Mary combined multiple forms of visual representation in a strategic manner throughout the lesson. Her first strategy was to provide students with diagrammatic representations of the human reproduction system (Figure 2). Devoid of gruesome biological details (blood and bodily fluids) or explicit references to organic elements (flesh, bones), these biologically "clean" diagrams are simpler for students to visualize than the highly detailed and realistic photography that followed. Use of such sanitized visuals from which the biological grotesque is systematically removed (Weinstein & Broda, 2009) can make biological content more readily accessible to students.

In this form of visual representation, the biological system is simplified or reduced to its essence, as only a few biological features are highlighted to viewers in a straightforward and often exaggerated manner. On diagrams, body parts can more easily be identified as students do not have to deal with the messiness of real samples or specimens whose biological features are not always clearly evident. Mary's second strategy was the use of a physical model, a more tangible and concrete representation composed of everyday objects with which students were familiar. During the PowerPoint presentation, Mary used a plastic bag with doll as representation for a baby inside a mother's uterus. Her reliance on the concrete and literal in support of ELLs is consistent with language educators' use of realia (Ash, Tellez, & Crain, 2009; Fathman & Crowther, 2006) and models (Weinburgh & Silva, 2011). Rather than simply expecting students to imagine, Mary sought to provide students with a means to directly observe what a fetus looks like inside the mother's uterus in tridimensional space.

Mary's use of multiple representations in support of ELLs can be understood as a measure aimed at preventing cognitive overload and promotion of germane load (optimized working memory load; Sweller, 2010). When students experience cognitive overload, they feel overwhelmed and have problems processing curricular information. In the specific case of ELLs, mental overload can be associated with language as well as content. When learning science, ELLs can experience cognitive overload as a result of an excessively high linguistic load as well as an excessively high conceptual load. Mary's use of diagrams and physical representations helped prevent cognitive overload by making biological content more accessible to students prior to engaging them in visual decoding, thus reducing the conceptual load of the dissection photographs. As a result, ELLs could devote their mental efforts to verbalizing visual features without having to also cope with the conceptual demands of the photos. Such an approach to visual decoding of scientific imagery can be understood as a tipped balance whose language load surpasses its cognitive load (Figure 3). This practice of providing ELLs with a simplified visual input and promoting student conceptual understanding before setting out to verbally codify more complex imagery serves specifically to address the CCSS visual demand for student engagement in image-to-word transformation of science content. Verbalizing images requires that students have a clear understanding of visually depicted science concepts, which teachers can promote via dialogic decoding of simplified images first.

## Visual Encoding

Visual encoding refers to classroom activities wherein students are asked to visually represent talk or text (that is, to turn spoken or written words into images). Students learn by creating a visual representation of verbally encoded science content. Although visual encoding also involves transmediation (Short, 2004), or transfer of content across representational media, information is

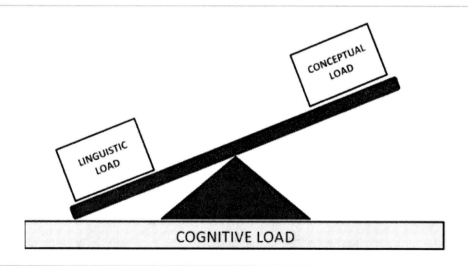

*Figure 3. Mary's Support of ELLs During Visual Decoding of Scientific Imagery*

Figure 4. *Students Constructing a Geologic Timeline With Adding Machine Tape*

transferred from texts to visuals, the reverse direction of visual decoding. Students engage in the production end of visual communication (as opposed to visual reception), and are guided by the teacher while learning to create visual representations according to scientific norms rather than reading scientific imagery produced by others.

This form of guided visualization was adopted by Karen, a ninth-grade teacher of earth science, during a lesson on the geologic timeline. Among her students were four ELLs with intermediate or higher levels of English proficiency. Karen's learning objectives for this particular lesson included having students collaboratively create a scale model of earth's history with its main eras (Pre-Cambrian, Paleozoic, Mesozoic, and Cenozoic) sequentially organized based on relative time, and to introduce students to the standard units utilized by scientists to measure geologic time (eon, era, period, and epoch; see Figure 4). In working together, students discuss the placement of the cards (visual/linguistic output) and physically move the cards as they come to consensus.

Karen described her lesson as follows:

While I was planning this lesson, I made an effort to particularly focus on the comprehensible input piece as well as on the interactive piece. I thought that focusing particularly on these two components would ensure that the abstract concepts and very difficult academic vocabulary in the lesson were accessible to the students and that students would have the opportunity to process and interpret the information presented . . . the vocabulary was introduced visually on an overhead as well as aurally and it was posted on the blackboard so that students could reference it at all times throughout the lesson. I feel like I used speech that was careful and deliberate and that the instructions were clear and explicit.

After providing directions to the whole class, Karen moved from group to group as she answered questions, pointed to specific parts or components, and helped students organize the layout of their timeline:

Karen: [To whole class] Today, we're going to make a timeline . . . basically what you'll be doing with your partner is you're going to get a sheet of adding machine tape. Do you guys even know what an adding machine is? This probably looks like [holding out a length of paper tape] a register tape to you, right? Like when you get a receipt at a store. You're going to be taking this with your partner and you're going to be measuring out a certain amount. You're going to be measuring based on the times you have on your worksheet the events that have occurred in the past . . . And the reason that we put the desks together is because it represents four and a half billion years. So we're talking about a very long period of time. Like I say in class, you can't pull up a lawn chair and watch erosion happen, or watch mountains get built up . . .

[To student pair A] My suggestion is, as you're facing your timeline, my suggestion is that you write "today" at the right end and the beginning of the Earth at the left end so that your timeline reads like a book.

[To student pair B] You can put "formation of the Earth" at the far left [waving her left hand] of your timeline . . . so the left edge is going to be the beginning of the Precambrian and the right end you're going to label "today." And then everything gets measured back from "today."

[To student pair C] Oh, you're going to have to color it. I recommend white for Precambrian, can you tell why [pointing to the timeline]? Look at Precambrian. So you're welcome to do pattern or a color if you like . . . Look at how much of your timeline is going to be Precambrian.

As can be seen in the transcript, Karen's interactions with her students center on how to visually represent textually encoded scientific information, namely the relative duration of geological eras as well as the age of important events in earth's past, such as the oldest known rocks, earliest trilobites, extensive coal forming forests, extinction of land and marine organisms, earliest dinosaurs, earliest birds, extinction of dinosaurs, and first humans. Based on fossilized records and other forms of geological evidence, this factual information was found in instructional texts, such as reference tables, in the students' science textbooks. Visual encoding of these temporal measurements required careful attention to be given to representational issues or attributes such as materiality, relative length, color coding, labeling, and directionality.

Karen's approach to visual encoding is consistent with model-based science teaching (Gilbert & Ireton, 2003; Glynn, 2008; Watkins, Miller, & Brubaker, 2004). In this pedagogical practice, an analog (simple and concrete) that shares certain features with a target concept (complex and intangible) serves as a representation or model and is used as a pedagogical device for simplifying and helping students visualize complex scientific phenomena. From this perspective, students' adding tape model serves as an analog for the target concept of geologic time. Further, the passing of time is depicted metaphorically as spatial movement (linear motion from left to right) along a straight line. The adding tape model constituted a spatial metaphor (Boroditsky, 2000) wherein the abstract and elusive domain of time was representationally extended and mapped onto the more concrete and comprehensible experiential domain of physical movement. This spatial metaphor provided Karen and the students with a more concrete means to talk about and organize scientific information about time.

Previous research has revealed varied conceptions of time among members of different cultures. Whorf (1956) describes how the Hopi conceive of time duration in terms of *cyclicity* (successive recurrences of events) rather than a quantifiable sequence of events along an imaginary straight line or row. Boroditsky (2001) reports that, while English speakers tend to think of time horizontally (unfolding from left to right), Mandarin Chinese conceive of it in terms of vertical spatial relations (up/down). There is also evidence of two alternative spatial metaphors for time in English: the ego-moving metaphor (the observer moves toward the future along a time line) and the time-moving metaphor (time itself moves toward the future like a river or conveyor belt while the observer remains stationary; Boroditsky, 2000; Gentner, Imai, & Boroditsky, 2002; Lakoff & Johnson, 1999). White (2007) distinguishes between absolute time (a literal conception of events in terms of absolute dates or numbers) and relative time (a metaphorical conception of events in terms of their relative position and sequencing along a timeline). Differences in one's temporal schema can lead not only to slower processing times but also distinct inferences about time (interpretations of back and front). This potential to create difficulties for science learners with diverse metaphorical conceptions of time highlights the importance of giving careful consideration to guided visualization strategies. As described above, the practice of visual encoding can serve as an important source of dialogic guidance whereby teachers can help increase ELLs' familiarity with specialized terminology prior to prompting them to make nonliteral use of physical space and constructing metaphoric visuals from specialized texts. As such, this pedagogical practice addresses specifically the CCSS visual demand for student engagement in word-to-image transformation of science content.

In an effort to offer linguistic support for her ELLs, Karen capitalized on a word wall, which she used to introduce keywords and to make them visually accessible to students (see Figure 5).

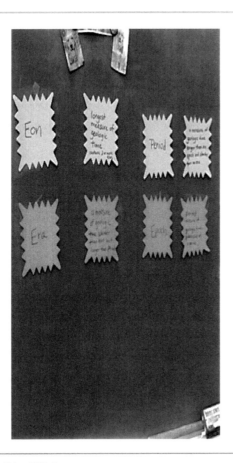

*Figure 5. Vocabulary on Karen's Word Wall*

This simple addition to her lesson greatly reduced the linguistic load by eliminating the need for students to have to remember on their own a set of specialized terms likely unfamiliar to them, such as *eons* and *epoch*. Having this terminology readily accessible through visual inspection of the classroom walls allowed students to focus on the content (that is, nonverbally portraying concepts) during visual encoding:

> Karen: So here's your vocabulary . . . because these words are so foreign to you, to all of us, I put them on the blackboard. So if you lose memory of what the different words mean you can get them off of the board. Okay so an eon is the longest measure of geologic time. So when they divide up all of the geologic time, which is how old is the earth's past, is called an eon. So that's like using a meter stick, and then we break it down into smaller amounts. The next time period that we measure is called an era, E-R-A, and this is the next smallest unit of measurement. So this might be like a half a meter. It would be like this [holding up a half-meter stick] if you can visualize this as being half of this [holding up a full meter stick]. So it's the next shortest measure of time . . . They then take an era and they divided those up into something called a period. So in my model I am showing you here [picking up the half meter stick] they are like the centimeters. So we're just taking a measurement and we're making it smaller and smaller. So a unit of geologic time longer than an epoch but shorter than an era . . . Then we have to break that down into something even smaller. We're going to divide this into a millimeter, which is even smaller than a centimeter. And we call those epochs, or "e-pox," I've heard people pronounce them both ways. The epoch is the shortest measure of geologic time.

Unlike Mary, who took a content-first approach (Brown & Ryoo, 2008) to guided visualization, Karen's support of ELLs centered on language first. By making the conventional meanings of temporal words explicit to students prior to their engagement in visual encoding, Karen promoted student comprehension on linguistic rather than conceptual grounds. In her class, provision of comprehensible input involved systematic reduction of linguistic load (that is, mental effort associated with the language of temporality) rather than sharing of prerequisite conceptual knowledge. Her approach to guided visualization can be understood as a tipped balance whose conceptual load surpasses its linguistic load (Figure 6). Karen sought to prevent her ELLs from experiencing cognitive overload by minimizing the mental effort needed to process specialized language used during visual encoding of geologic time.

Although clearly distinct in terms of their emphasis on the reduction of conceptual load or linguistic load when guiding ELLs' visualization of science concepts, the two approaches also had noticeable similarities. Both teachers sought to make the science content being visualized more relatable and comprehensible by strategically drawing upon students' prior experiences and previous knowledge. For instance, Mary started her lesson by facilitating an extended whole-class discussion about prenatal care. She posed the question "What does prenatal care mean?" and then encouraged students to share their ideas and opinions with regard to various issues, such as harmful substances from which mothers should abstain during the prenatal period. Likewise, when introducing the keywords on the word wall, Karen made a brief parenthetical remark on a popular movie: "How many people have ever heard of *Jurassic Park*? That's a time period, that's when dinosaurs lived. Awesome

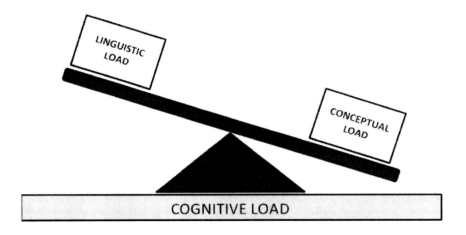

*Figure 6. Karen's Support of ELLs During Visual Encoding of Geologic Time*

movie, you should see it, check it out. That's one of the time periods from the past. It actually got its name from a real geologic time period." The students then responded to her questions about dinosaurs and their extinction. In both classrooms, teachers attempted to relate science content to students' everyday lives and to make content more meaningful and personally relevant.

In conclusion, guided visualization can provide science teachers with an effective means to promote ELLs' science literacies through images, and thus meet the visual demands of the CCSS. As demonstrated by Mary and Karen, teacher-led visual decoding of increasingly complex science visuals can provide ELLs with conceptual understandings needed to perform image-to-word transformations, whereas teacher-led visual encoding can provide ELLs with the specialized language necessary for the transformation of science texts into metaphoric visuals. Further, carefully implemented visual encoding and decoding activities can enable teachers to socialize ELLs into the visual cultural of science, which is characterized by the predominance of inscriptions (Latour & Woolgar, 1986)—highly abstract imagery devoid of realistic details and with a high degree of detachment from its original context of visual production (diagrams and graphs). As such, guided visualization can serve as a powerful pedagogical tool that teachers can use to promote ELLs' representational competence and inscription literacy, regardless of linguistic or cultural background.

## Reflection Questions and Action Plans

We would like you to examine your science textbook and supplementary materials for examples of how the discipline of science that you teach uses natural language and visual representation. The following reflective questions can help guide you as you consider your ELLs and their special literacy needs.

### Reflection Questions

1. Select two visual representations (perhaps a graph and a drawing) that are found in the textbook adopted by your school/district. What activity could you use to help your students explain what the representations are communicating (decoding)?

2. What resources can you use to help support the development of multiple literacies (particularly visualization) with your students?

3. What small variation in a basic lesson did Mary or Karen use that you would like to try? What made this aspect interesting to you?

## Action Plans

1. Collect different types of representations and highlight key visual attributes of images. Prepare a mini-lesson on how to read these visuals and what information they communicate that is not possible with natural language.

2. Mark more difficult diagrams in your textbook so that you will stop during your lesson to discuss the visual features of analytical diagrams to help students navigate illustrations.

3. Find a concept that is described in your text that you can teach as an encoding activity for your students. Be sure to think about the language support that students will need.

# References

Ainsworth, S., Prain, V., & Tytler, R. (2011). Drawing to learn in science. *Science, 333*, 1096–1097.

Ametller, J., & Pinto, R. (2002). Students' reading of innovative images of energy at secondary school level. *International Journal of Science Education, 24*, 285–312.

Ash, D., Tellez, K., & Crain, R. (2009). The importance of objects in talking science: The special case of English language learners. In K. R. Bruna & K. Gomez (Eds.), *The work of language in multicultural classrooms: Talking science, writing science.* New York, NY: Routledge.

Boroditsky, L. (2000). Metaphoric structuring: Understanding time through spatial metaphors. *Cognition, 75*, 1–28.

Boroditsky, L. (2001). Does language shape thought? Mandarin and English speakers' conceptions of time. *Cognitive Psychology, 43*, 1–22.

Brown, B. A., & Ryoo, K. (2008). Teaching science as language: A "content-first" approach to science teaching. *Journal of Research in Science Teaching, 45*(5), 529–553.

Catley, K. F., Novick, L. R., & Shade, C. K. (2010). Interpreting evolutionary diagrams: When topology and process conflict. *Journal of Research in Science Teaching, 47*(7), 861–882.

Fathman, A. K., & Crowther, D. T. (Eds.). (2006). *Science for English language learners: K–12 classroom strategies.* Arlington, VA: NSTA Press.

Gee, J. P. (2004). *Situated language and learning: A critique of traditional schools.* New York, NY: Routledge.

Gentner, D., Imai, M., & Boroditsky, L. (2002). As time goes by: Evidence for two systems in processing space→time metaphors. *Language and Cognitive Processes, 17*, 537–565.

Gilbert, J. K., Reiner, M., & Nakhleh, M. (Eds.). (2008). *Visualization: Theory and practice in science education.* New York, NY: Springer.

Gilbert, S. W., & Ireton, S. W. (2003). *Understanding models in earth and space science.* Arlington, VA: NSTA press.

Glynn, S. M. (2008). Making science concepts meaningful to students: Teaching with analogies. In S. Mikelskis-Seifert, U. Ringelband, & M. Bruckmann (Eds.), *Four decades of research in science education: From curriculum development to quality improvement* (pp. 112–125). Munster, Germany: Waxmann.

Kress, G., & van Leeuwen, T. (2006). *Reading images: The grammar of visual design* (2nd ed.). New York, NY: Routledge.

Lakoff, G., & Johnson, M. (1999). *Philosophy in the flesh: The embodied mind and its challenge to western thought.* New York, NY: Basic Books.

Latour, B., & Woolgar, S. (1986). *Laboratory life: The social construction of scientific facts* (2nd ed.). Princeton, NJ: Princeton University Press.

Lave, J., & Wenger, E. (1991). *Situated learning: Legitimate peripheral participation.* New York, NY: Cambridge University Press.

Lehesvuori, S., Viiri, J., Rasku-Puttonen, H., Moate, J., & Helaakoski, J. (2013). Visualizing communication structures in science classrooms: Tracing cumulatively in teacher-led whole class discussions. *Journal of Research in Science Teaching, 50*(8), 912–939.

Lemke, J. (1998). Multiplying meaning: Visual and verbal semiotics in scientific text. In J. R. Martin & R. Veel (Eds.), *Reading Science* (pp. 87–113). London, United Kingdom: Routledge.

Lemke, J. L. (2004). The literacies of science. In. E. W. Saul (Ed.). *Crossing borders in literacy and science instruction* (pp. 33–47). Arlington, VA: NSTA Press.

National Governors' Association Center for Best Practices & Council of Chief State School Officers. (2010). *Common Core State Standards for English language arts and literacy in history/social studies, science, and technical subjects.* Washington, DC: Authors. http://www.corestandards.org

NGSS Lead States. (2013). *Next Generation Science Standards: For states, by states.* Washington, DC: The National Academies Press.

Roth, W.-M. (2004). Gestures: The leading edge in literacy development. In. E. W. Saul (Ed.), *Crossing borders in literacy and science instruction* (pp. 48–68). Arlington, VA: NSTA Press.

Roth, W.-M. (2008). Bricolage, metissage, hybridity, heterogeneity, diaspora: Concepts for thinking science education in the 21st century. *Cultural Studies of Science Education, 3,* 891–916.

Roth, W.-M. (2014). Science language wanted alive: Through the dialectical/dialogical lens of Vygotsky and the Bakhtin Circle. *Journal of Research in Science Teaching, 51*(8), 1049–1083.

Short, K. G. (2004). Researching intertextuality within collaborative learning environments. In N. Shuart-Faris & D. Bloome (Eds.), *Uses of intertextuality in classroom and educational research* (pp. 373–396). Greenwich, CT: Information Age.

Sturken, M., & Cartwright, L. (2009). *Practices of looking: An introduction to visual culture.* New York, NY: Oxford University Press.

Sweller, J. (2010). Element interactivity and intrinsic, extraneous and germane cognitive load. *Educational Psychology Review, 22,* 123–138.

Vasquez, J., Comer, M., & Troutman, F. (2010). *Developing visual literacy in science, K–8.* Arlington, VA: NSTA Press.

Watkins, J. K., Miller, E., & Brubaker, D. (2004). The role of visual image: What are students really learning from pictorial representations? *Journal of Visual Literacy, 24,* 23–40.

Weinburgh, M. H., & Silva, C. (2011). Math, science, and models. *Science & Children, 48*(10), 38–42.

Weinstein, M., & Broda, M. (2009). Resuscitating the critical in the biological grotesque: Blood, guts, biomachismo in science/education and human guinea pig discourse. *Cultural Studies of Science Education, 4,* 761–780.

White, O. (2007). *An investigation into the utilization of a constructivist teaching strategy to improve preservice elementary teachers' geological content knowledge: Is there a relationship between intellectual level and content of understanding?* (Unpublished doctoral dissertation). Indiana University Bloomington.

Whorf, B. L. (1956). The relation of habitual thought and behavior to language. In J. B. Caroll (Ed.), *Language, thought and reality: Selected writings of Benjamin Lee Whorf* (pp. 134–159). Cambridge, MA: MIT Press.

Yore, L. D. (2004). Why do future scientists need to study the language arts? In. E. W. Saul (Ed.), *Crossing borders in literacy and science instruction* (pp. 71–94). Arlington, VA: NSTA Press.

# CONTENT-AREA
# INTEGRATION

# Reader-Culture-Text Mergence: Seven Pedagogical Principles

*Ann M. Johns, San Diego State University*

A major strength of the Common Core State Standards (CCSS; National Governors Association Center for Best Practices [NGA] & Council of Chief State School Officers [CCSSO], 2010) is its directive to teachers across the curriculum that they must be literacy specialists in their own content areas. Squire (2011) tells us that

> the CCSS take a clear stand on behalf of reading and writing across the curriculum. The insistence on making reading and writing instruction "a shared responsibility" within schools signals that teachers in multiple disciplines will be expected to help foster literacy development . . . (p. 15)

Drawing from research into the disciplinary literacies, analyses of the CCSS, the best practices literature, as well as my own experiences (Johns, in press-a, in press-b), I will first claim that this mandate requires content-area teachers to reject the argument for "general academic English" and instead teach the CCSS standards as they are realized in their own disciplinary cultures. For, as Wray (2002) notes:

> Each subject discipline constitutes a way of making sense of human experience that has evolved over generations and each is dependent on its own particular practices: its instrumental procedures, its criteria for judging relevance and validity, and its conventions of acceptable forms of argument. In a word, each has developed its own modes of discourse. (p. 290)

My second, considerably different, claim is based upon the knowledge that the CCSS reading standards focus almost exclusively on careful text analysis ("inside the text"), not on what the student may bring to text personally, linguistically, or culturally to reading and writing. For this reason, the following skills and strategies are central to the standards:

- In argumentation: Identify various types of evidence made for a claim, and, in higher grade levels, evaluate the use of that evidence. Evaluate the premises upon which an argument is made. Solve a problem, based upon evaluation of evidence or premises.

- Summarize different types of texts, relying on text structures and other features.

- Locate key facts about a scientific phenomenon. Identify details or key ideas. Analyze hierarchical arrangements in scientific texts.

- Make distinctions among ideas within separate texts.

- Integrate information from more than one source using synthesis, determining central ideas from more than one text.

What is missing? Calkins, Ehrenworth, and Lehman (2012) note that the CCSS omit the reader elements, including ". . . text-to-self connections, access to prior knowledge, exploring personal response, and relating texts to your own life. In short, the Common Core deemphasizes reading as a personal act and emphasizes textual analysis" (p. 25).

It seems clear, then, that teachers must create pedagogies that build bridges between the "text-internal" (or "understanding a text on its own terms"; Newkirk, 2013, p. 23) requirements of the CCSS and the needs, backgrounds, and experiences of the students. In this chapter, this "bridges" approach to classroom pedagogy is called reader-culture-text mergence (RCTM).

## The Common Core State Standards and Specific Demands on ELLs

### Special Challenges

Though it is clear that there are many challenges facing ELLs and their teachers (e.g., see Ramirez, 2015), two particularly important areas will be the focus of this chapter: the text-internal CCSS emphasis and, as a result, repairing the discordances between the CCSS literacies focus and ELL students' experiences, needs, and motivations.

First, what is meant by "text-internal"? An official statement on student reading, produced by NGA, co-initiators of the CCCS, tells us what this means:

Students who meet the standards readily undertake the *close, attentive reading* [emphasis added] that is at the heart of understanding and enjoying complex works. . . . They *habitually* [emphasis added] perform the critical reading necessary *to pick carefully* [emphasis added] through the staggering amount of information available today in print and digitally. (NGA & CCSSO, 2010, p. 3)

Where do we start with the challenges of text-internal reading for ELLs? In his review of the research, Grabe (2004) highlights the importance of an extensive vocabulary for accurate reading in

English (p. 47), quoting Carver (2003) as saying that "the relationship between text comprehension and vocabulary knowledge is so strong that research can produce perfect correlations" (p. 153). For the CCSS, student readers need to know explicit word meanings as well as those that are figurative and inexplicit. A second text-internal area challenging for ELLs is recognizing text structures, signaled by features that include transition words, topic sentences, and definite reference to prior text ideas as well as headings and visuals (Duke & Pearson, 2002). Because unconventional structures are also factors in text complexity, strategies for analysis are crucial for successful comprehension.

Are ELLs given well-scaffolded activities that enable them to engage in the "picky" analysis of complex texts? Not always, for a number of reasons (see Karabenick & Clemens Noda, 2004). Brooks (2015), in a multilayered study of reading teaching, discovered that rather than being encouraged to draw from their own lives before, during, and after reading, the ELLs in some California classrooms experienced something quite different: The teacher or monolingual English students read texts aloud, and then the teacher lectured the class on what the texts meant. Due to these top-down instructional practices, the Latino students instructed conceived of "reading" in this way:

1. *Effective reading means fluent oral reading of texts* [emphasis added]: "Good readers do not stumble over words, stutter, misread words, read in a low voice, or read slowly."

2. *Comprehension of a reading is quick and easy* [emphasis added]: "Good readers immediately understand what they read."

3. *Those proficient readers who read aloud and those listening to readers know how to act in a classroom* [emphasis added]: "Good readers behave like 'good' students." (Brooks, 2015, pp. 399–400)

Also focusing on instruction for ELLs, Athanases and de Oliveira (2010) examined scaffolding for literacies in a California secondary school. What they found was that "routine scaffolding," which focused principally on "picking carefully through texts," as the CCSS assessments require, was less effective than scaffolding that also drew from students' own experiences with texts and first languages as well as from their cultures and educational lives (see also Drucker, 2003). Though historically there have been strict boundaries in many schools established between students lives—and especially their first languages and cultures—and English language teaching (Cook, 2001), it is now believed by many researchers and practitioners that drawing from texts the students themselves have written, their lives, and their languages, can be very beneficial (McMillan & Rivers, 2011; see also Celic & Seltzer, 2011, on "translanguaging").

## Rationale

### Linguistic Variation in the Content Areas

Drawing from large corpora, researchers have identified distinct vocabulary differences among disciplinary texts. Hyland and Tse (2007), for example, point out that "even the same words have different frequencies, collocations and different meanings across fields" (p. 235). They found that the most common terms used across the disciplines are *analysis* and *process*; however, what these words mean—and what the words do—for and within academic texts varies across the content areas. CCSS writers agree. Reading Anchor Standard 1 for Grades 6–12, for example, tells students to "cite specific textual evidence" (NGA & CCSSO, 2010, p. 35). However, in science, typical evidence is found in current "science and technical texts" (RST.6–12.1; p. 62). In history, on the other hand, the evidence appears in "primary and secondary sources" (RH.6–12.1; p. 61). So, though a so-called cross-disciplinary term is employed in both cases, the types of texts from which the evidence is selected, and the evidence itself, will vary, as the content standards listed indicate.

*Process*, too, differs in its use across the content areas. For science and technology, students "*follow precisely a multistep procedure* [emphasis added] when carrying out experiments" (RST.6–8.3; p. 62). Conversely, in history/social studies, students "identify key steps in a text's description of a process" (RH.6–8.3). For the science students, then, there are preconceived multistep procedures, but history students must discover the "key [process] steps" in other ways, textual moves that may differ significantly from one source to another, depending on the genre, the writer, the historical period, and other factors.

Other linguistic distinctions among the content areas are seen in "formulaic sequences": predictable three-, four-, or five-word clusters (Peters & Pauwels, 2015), which are said to represent as much as 80% of academic language. Hyland (2008), in a study of published articles and masters theses, developed a classification system for these sequences, which he calls "lexical bundles," placing them into three categories: research oriented, which enable writers to assist readers in understanding the studies proposed or completed; text oriented, which alert readers to transitions in the text and to how the text is structured; and participant-oriented, which show a writer's attitude toward a topic or address readers directly. Not surprisingly, there is variation in the distribution of these sequences across the disciplines. Here are the frequently occurring formulaic sequences in history and social studies, using the CCSS. Sequence examples are in parentheses and italics:

### History

Grades 6–8: . . . text presents information sequentially (*first, second, third; then, next; in the next section*); comparatively (*like xx, yy is written as prose; in contrast to yy, xx is well-known*); causally (*because this happened, this happened; as a result of*).

Grades 9–10: . . . emphasize key points (*this is important because; it should be noted that*); advance an explanation of analysis (*a further point is; as we shall see*).

Grades 11–12: . . . show how a complex primary source is structured, including how key sentences (*at the beginning; be found in the*), paragraphs, and larger portions of the text contribute to the whole (*in such a way; in the context of; in the same way*).

### Science

Grades 6–8: Analyze the structure . . . to organize a text, including how the major sections (*in the next section; one of the main; the position of the*) contribute to the whole and to an understanding of the topic (*may be used to; the purpose of the*).

Grades 9–10: . . . the structure of the relationships among concepts in a text, including relationships among key terms (*to be found in; may be due to; be related to the*).

---

**Reading Standard 5: History/Social Studies**

RH.6–8.5: Describe how a text presents information (e.g., sequentially, comparatively, causally).

RH.9–10.5: Analyze how a text uses structure to emphasize key points or advance an explanation or analysis.

RH.11–12.5: Analyze in detail how a complex primary source is structured, including how key sentences, paragraphs, and larger portions of the text contribute to the whole.

**Reading Standard 5: Science and Technology**

RST.6–8.5: Analyze the structure an author uses to organize a text, including how the major sections contribute to the whole and an understanding of the topic.

RST.9–10.5: Analyze the structure of the relationships among concepts in a text, including relationships among key terms (e.g., *force, friction, reaction force, energy*).

RST.11–12.5: Analyze how the text structures information or ideas into categories or hierarchies, demonstrating understanding of the information or ideas.

*Figure. Reading Standard 5, Examples From History/Social Studies and Science/Technology (NGA & CCSSO, 2010)*

Grades 11–12: . . . the text structures information or ideas into categories or hierarchies (*at the level of; between two groups; levels are connected in the sense that*) . . .

As can be seen, the requirements of the content standards, for example "structure of the relationships among concepts in a text," often result in the use of lexical bundles such as "to be found in," or "may be due to."

# Pedagogical Practice: Seven Pedagogical Principles for Reader-Culture-Text Mergence Approach

The purpose of the RCTM approach is to narrow the gap between the "picky" within-the-text focus of the CCSS across the content areas and the life experiences of the ELLs. These general principles that pursue this goal should be in play throughout the year and are outlined here. Two texts (Appendices A and B) were selected as exemplars for this section because they are from the same genre (book review), are accessible, and cover topics from history/social studies that should be of interest to students in middle and high schools. A few of many activities supporting the principles are presented here.

## Principle 1: Draw From Students' Prior Knowledge or Lived Experiences

As previously noted, Athanases and de Oliveira (2010) found that relating academic work to ELLs' lives is considerably more motivating than routine scaffolding. Visual material is very important to certain disciplines (see Johns, 1998), and it can elicit interesting and creative ideas from students' experiences about almost any text to be read—in this case, in preparation for approaching *Mendiz v.*

*Westminister* (Appendix A). The activity below is adapted from Smith, Appleman, and Wilhelm (2014, pp. 48–49):

- Post pictures around the room that portray a poorly appointed classroom, with shoddy furniture and little decoration. In the pictures, only Latino students are in attendance.

- Ask students to complete a "gallery walk" of these pictures, then, in groups, to guess the answers to these questions:

  1. Who are these people? Where are they?

  2. What is their situation? Are they happy, sad? Why?

  3. What do you think that their problems or challenges are?

  4. Can you think of other groups of students who may have had similar experiences? [Some students may know about the de jure segregation of African American children.]

  5. What experiences have you had with feeling separated from other groups of students? How have these made you feel?

After students write a short reflection on what they saw in these pictures, they read silently paragraphs 2–3 of the Appendix A text that tells the story of Latino segregation and the lawsuit filed against this practice. In a history class, this story can lead to a short written piece in which issues around *Brown vs. the Board of Education* are compared and contrasted with those that ensued in the Mendez case.

## Principle 2: Encourage Different Types of Predictions

A considerable number of activities are available for prereading, generally anticipating content or concepts in a text (see Fisher, Brozo, Frey, & Ivey, 2011); however, there are other features of texts relating to genre, author purposes, text structure, and student experiences that can help ELLS to expand their schemas for the variety of texts to which they will be exposed, or required to write, across the content areas.

For this activity, using Table 1, students can be divided into groups, each with a different copy of Table 1, without any of the columns completed. One group completes the table using the text in Appendix A; the second group also completes the table, and uses the text in Appendix B (from the same genre: the book review). This activity can be followed by comparing the two sets of predictions by the entire class.

## Principle 3: Help Students to Establish Reading (and Writing) Purposes, Based Upon the Standards (and Assessments)

As has already been discussed, the standards are text-internal, so examining internal features of the text should be central to lessons across the curriculum. As Calkins and her colleagues (2012) point out, teachers in the content areas need to provide students with strategies for engaging with and responding to these text-internal standards (pp. 29–31).

## Table 1. Prediction Grid

| | Predictions |
|---|---|
| 1. What is this type of text called? (Its genre name) | |
| 2. What are predicable author purposes? Why did the author write it? | |
| 3. Who might write a text like this? Why? If a teacher or student wrote this, what content area would s/he be from? | |
| 4. How might the text be organized? That is, what would be talked about first, second, third . . . OR What functions might the paragraphs serve? (E.g., to define, tell a story, summarize . . .) | |
| 5. Is there anything in or around the text that will help you to read it? | |

How might this be done? Let's take Standard 6 for Grades 9–10, history/social studies as an example:

RH.9–10.6
Compare the point of view of two or more authors for how they treat the same or similar topics, including which details they include and emphasize in their respective accounts.

- Teachers work with the students to convert this standard into a set of tasks that are manageable, encouraging them to do as much of the standard analysis as possible. In pairs, they answer one or more these questions and then share with the class:

  — What are the key words in the listed standard (above)?

  — If you were trying to respond to this standard using our readings (Appendices A and B), what actions would you take first? Second? Third? (e.g., "First, we would read both texts carefully. Then, we would list, compare, and contrast the details in each text.")

  — What points or ideas would a paper that responds to this standard need to include, working with our readings (Appendices A and B)?

  — What writing prompt covers the requirements of the standard? (Together with the teacher, students prepare a writing prompt that includes all the key words and directions in the standard.)

I have found that this approach gives students considerable control over how they respond to a text-internal standard. It becomes their own, rather than some abstract set of instructions from a testing agency.

## Principle 4: Encourage Careful Selection and Organization of Vocabulary

There is no doubt that vocabulary is essential to proficient academic literacies (e.g., Zwiers, 2005; Anderson, 1999; Grabe, 2004). However, students can be overwhelmed by unfamiliar words if teachers don't limit what is taught or provide for opportunities to draw from prior knowledge and predict before they turn to words in a text. And even then, words actually selected for teaching, in contrast to those discovered by the students, should be few, according to Kinsella (2011). How can we help students to limit and work with vocabulary in a manageable way?

- **Organizing words by function:** Post words or phrases, preferably discovered by the students from texts, in categories that serve related functions, for example, citation words or metadiscourse (words and phrases that lead the reader through the text). Students are encouraged to add words to a category when they appear in a text (In Appendices A and B, the metadiscourse includes: *ultimately*; *in other words*; *and yet*.)

- **Focusing on content-area word use:** In the sciences, there are word hierarchies (*genus*, *species*, etc.). These can be organized in visuals, as the discipline requires, or the words can be classified in other ways. Here, for example, are tasks related to the exemplar texts:

  — List and then categorize (in any way that seems reasonable to you) all of the words in the texts that relate to law or the American court system.

  — List and (look up) synonyms for words or phrases the author uses to evaluate the book being reviewed.

  — Underline and list the words (or the grammatical features) that show that a section of the text is a narrative.

- **Locating author word choices in a text:** Because the standards emphasize the role of a term in a specific text (Anchor Standard 4), students can identify and discuss why the author made certain lexical choices. In Appendix B, for example, students might discuss "egregious" (para 4) or "xenophobic" (para 6) and argue for why the author used these words, considering other possibilities among synonyms.

- **Drawing on prior linguistic knowledge:** Encourage students who speak Romance languages such as Spanish, French, or Italian to notice what is familiar about English words and list possible cognates. In Appendix A, students would find "facility" (*facilidad* in Spanish), "separate" (*separar* in Spanish), and "uniquely" (*unico* in Italian or Spanish), for instance. The concept of translanguaging, the use of bilingualism as a resource, is important for these students because through their first languages they can come to know English more easily (see Celic & Seltzer, 2011).

## Principle 5: Provide "Repeated, Distributed Practice"

Willingham (2009), a noted psychologist, tells us that we need to ask students to practice strategy activities (with a variety of texts) until they have developed a certain amount of automaticity. How, for example, can we provide repeated, distributed practice in determining text structures as emphasized in CCSS Anchor Standards 3 and 5? Making use of the activities they have already completed (above, from Principles 1–4), students can now chart the texts in Appendices A and B using Table 2.

- Teachers need to preread a text and prepare a grid similar to Table 2 that is appropriate. Sometimes, several paragraphs have the same function, so the teacher needs to number or group the paragraphs accordingly before the students begin the activity.

- Then, using Table 2 and one of the readings, groups decide what the author is doing (his or her intent) in each of the numbered paragraphs/sections in the text; that is, what the paragraph's functions are (first column). The second column, "How do you know?", is in this table because it's important for students to consider the language used that indicates the author's purpose(s). The third column asks for a summary of the paragraph(s).

## Table 2. Charting the Text
### (Partially Completed Example, Using Appendix A)

| Para # | What is the author doing? | How do you know (what the author is doing)? What language tells you this? | What is the author saying? (A summary) |
|---|---|---|---|
| 1 | a. Focusing on book's importance <br> b. Evaluating the writing | a. "Finally, giving Mendez its due" <br> b. "a concise and compelling account . . . while retaining its essential human face" | |
| 2 | a. Narrating the book's story <br> b. Telling why these children were discriminated against | a. "In 1945," use of the past tense <br> b. . . ."based on ancestry and supposed 'language deficiency'" | |
| 3 | Focusing on the court's decision . . . more of the book's story | "Judge Paul McCormick came to support the plaintiffs" | |
| 4 | Identifying support for the court's decision; showing the later importance of this case | . . . supported by . . . leading civil liberties organizations . . . the NAACP "which would adapt the arguments . . . in Brown" | |
| 5 | a. Evaluating the writing <br> b. Showing approval of the author's point of view | a. ". . . effectively weaves together narrative and analysis . . ." <br> b. ". . . presents issues evenhandedly" | |
| 6 | a. Summarizing the importance of the Mendez case <br> b. Applying importance to today | a. | |

Because this activity, which should be repeated, may be new to some readers, Table 2 shows what the groups might conclude for columns 2 and 3, using the text in Appendix A. This type of activity is useful for a number of Reading (and certainly Writing) Anchor Standards in the CCSS: Standard 1, requiring students to understand and summarize exactly what's in the text; Standard 5, relating specifically to text structure; or Standard 3, which refers to the "unfolding" of the text. (See LiteracyTA.com for related activities.)

## Principle 6: Create Opportunities for Short Writings Based on the Readings

Both the constructed responses and the performance tasks of the CCSS assessments require fairly short written pieces based on sources, though, of course, the final paper for the performance task is longer. It's important that students write from different types of text (visual and print) often, and under timed conditions, so that they can practice for the CCSS assessments and prepare for college assessments (see Melzer, 2014). For these reasons, the "charting" activities can be followed by a writing prompt such as: "How does the author of the *Mendez v Westminster* review develop his claims? What impact does this structure have upon you, the reader?"

## Principle 7: Allow Ample Time for Critique and Reflection

It has been established by considerable research (e.g., Cadieux, 2012; Wirth & Aziz, 2009) that developing metacognitive awareness (thinking about, and regulating, one's own thinking and strategizing) is of considerable use for the development of schemata and reading comprehension. Nonetheless, as noted earlier, "the Common Core deemphasizes reading as a personal act" (Calkins, Ehrenworth, & Lehman, 2012, p. 25). For this reason, teachers need to fill this gap by providing opportunities for student critique and reflection. Here are a few questions, used individually, that have been given to students for short beginning or end-of-class reflections on one or more readings:

**About reading strategies**
- What prior knowledge assisted you in reading this text? What did you need to know and how did you come to know it?

- How did you approach the reading of this (new) text? What did you do first, second, and third? Did you repeat any strategies? Did these strategies for reading help you to comprehend better? Why or why not?

- What parts or elements of the reading were most difficult for you? What parts did you find to be fairly easy to read (if any)?

- What did you learn from the text that you might share with someone else?

**About the text itself**
- Where do you think this text was written? When?

- What would you call this text (genre)?

- Who was the text written for? How do you know? In what content area would be it found?

- What was the author's purpose? What was his/her point of view?

- Would you recommend this reading to another student? Why or why not?

- What is an appropriate one-sentence summary of the text?

**Text critique**
- Did you like this reading? Why or why not?

- Did the author help you to visualize anything in the text?

- Did you like the author? Would you like to be his/her friend or relative?

- Is the text well written? Why or why not?

- What will you, as a reader and individual, take from the experience of reading this text?

# Reflection Questions and Action Plans

## Reflection Questions

1. What ideas or activities will you take from this chapter and apply to your classrooms? Why? Of what use to your students will they be, if any?

2. In what ways, if any, will this chapter be helpful to you in your professional life?

3. The author claims that "there is no general English." Do you accept this claim? If so, why? If not, why not? Will this claim be useful in your teaching—or not?

4. The author cites Grabe (2004), who draws from the research to point out that issues of vocabulary and text structure seem to be two of the most challenging for ELL reading. Do you disagree? If so, what are the greatest challenges? If you agree, what activities would you add to the ones suggested in this chapter?

5. It could be argued that English/ELA teachers may not be the best people to lead CCSS professional development workshops. Do you believe this is true? Why or why not? What stand does your school take on this issue?

## Action Plans

1. Try out one or more of the activities suggested in this chapter with your students. What worked? What didn't? What had to be modified for your classroom?

2. Ask your students to examine a text (from their home communities) for its "rhetorical context," that is, where it was written/created or published, who wrote it, and for whom. Encourage them to find out what was going on when the text was written.

3. Ask your students to focus on the author's ethos, or credibility, in a text. What in the text or the author's background gives the author the credibility to write it? What did they know about the author before reading that might give him or her credibility? What is the tone of the text? How does the tone relate to the author's ethos and purposes?

4. Try out one or more activities in this chapter that relate to the students' own "homely" texts (Miller, 1984). Are the students more motivated when they can select the texts from their own contexts and in their own languages? Do they have more insights that will help them to be the kinds of critical thinkers that the CCSS require?

5. One useful genre for text analysis is the opinion editorial. Select one that deals with a controversial topic (e.g., What should be done about bullying? Should older students be able to carry guns?) Ask students to use some of the activities in this chapter to analyze the text, with particular emphasis on the author's point of view (Anchor Standard 6). In a short paper, ask students to explain the author's point of view and then compare/contrast it with their own.

# References

Anderson, N. (1999). *Exploring second language reading.* Boston, MA: Heinle & Heinle.

Athanases, S. Z., & de Oliveira, L. C. (2010). Toward program-wide coherence in preparing teachers to teach and advocate for English language learners. In T. Lucas (Ed.), *Teacher preparation for linguistically diverse classrooms: A resource for teacher educators* (pp. 195–215). New York, NY: Routledge.

Brooks, M. D. (2015). "It's like a script": Long-term English learners' experiences with and ideas about academic reading. *Research in the Teaching of English, 49,* 383–406.

Cadieux, C. (2012, March 30). Reading reflection can boost reading comprehension [Web log]. Retrieved from http://info.marygrove.edu/MATblog/bid/80719/Reading-reflection-can-boost-reading -comprehension.

Calkins, L., Ehrenworth, M., & Lehman, C. (2012). *Pathways to the Common Core: Accelerating achievement.* Portsmouth, NH: Heinemann.

Carver, R. (2003). The highly lawful relationships among pseudoword decoding, word identification, spelling, listening, and reading. *Scientific Studies of Reading, 7,* 127–154.

Celic, C., & Seltzer, K. (2011). *Translanguaging: A CUNY-NYSIEB guide for educators.* New York, NY: CUNY-NYSIEB. Retrieved from http://www.nysieb.ws.gc.cuny.edu/files/2012/06/FINAL-Translanguaging-Guide -With-Cover-1.pdf

Cook, V. (2001). Using the first language in the classroom. *Canadian Modern Language Review, 27,* 402–423.

Drucker, M. J. (2003). What reading teachers should know about ESL learners. *The Reading Teacher, 57,* 22–29.

Duke, N., & Pearson, P. D. (2002). Effective practices for developing reading comprehension. *Journal of Education, 189,* 107–122.

Fisher, D., Brozo, W. G., Frey, N., & Ivey, G. (2011). *50 instructional routines to develop content literacy* (2nd ed.). Boston, MA: Pearson Education.

Freedman, R. (2014). *Angel Island: Gateway to Gold Mountain.* New York, NY: Clarion.

Grabe, W. (2004). Research on teaching reading. *Annual Review of Applied Linguistics, 24,* 44–69.

Hyland, K. (2008). As can be seen: Lexical bundles and disciplinary variation. *English for Specific Purposes, 27,* 4–21.

Hyland, K., & Tse, P. (2007). Is there an "academic vocabulary"? *TESOL Quarterly, 41,* 235–254.

Johns, A. M. (1998). The visual and the verbal: A case study in macroeconomics. *English for Specific Purposes, 17,* 183–198.

Johns, A. M. (in press-a). The Common Core in the United States: A major shift in standards and assignments. In K. Hyland & P. Shaw (Eds.), *Routledge handbook of English for academic purposes.* London, England: Routledge.

Johns, A. M. (in press-b). Students as genre scholars: ESL/EFL approaches. In N. Artemeva & A. Freedman (Eds.), *Trends and traditions in genre studies.* Ardrossan, Alberta, Canada: Inkshed Publications.

Karabenick, S. A., & Clemens Noda, P. A. (2004). Professional development implications of teachers' beliefs and attitudes toward English language learners. *Bilingual Research Journal, 28,* 55–75.

LiteracyTA.com. (n.d.). Analyzing text structure. Retrieved from http://www.literacyta.com/literacy-skills /analyzing-text-structure?nocache=1

McMillan, B. A., & Rivers, D. J. (2011). The practice of policy: Teacher attitudes toward "English-only." *Systems, 39*(2), 251–263.

Melzer, D. (2014). *Assignments across the curriculum: A national study of college writing.* Logan, UT: Utah State University Press.

Miller, C. (1984). Genre as social action. *Quarterly Journal of Speech, 70,* 151–167.

National Governors' Association Center for Best Practices & Council of Chief State School Officers. (2010). *Common Core State Standards for English language arts and literacy in history/social studies, science, and technical subjects.* Washington, DC: Authors. http://www.corestandards.org

Newkirk, T. (2013). *Speaking back to the Common Core.* Portsmouth, NH: Heinemann.

Partington, R. (2013, November). Angel Island. Retrieved from http://richiespicks.pbworks.com/w/page /67570942/angel%20island

Peters, E., & Pauwels, P. (2015). Learning academic formulaic sequences. *Journal of English for Academic Purposes, 20,* 28–39.

Ramirez, M. (2015, June 16). For teachers of English learners, Common Core means double the work. Retrieved from http://hechingerreport.org/for-teachers-of-english-learners-common-core-means-double -the-work/

Smith, M. W., Appleman, D., & Wilhelm, J. D. (2014). *The uncommon core: Where the authors of the standards go wrong about instruction—and how you can get it right.* Thousand Oaks, CA: Corwin Press.

Squire, J. R. (March, 2011). Reading and writing across the curriculum: A NCTE policy research brief. *Council Chronicle.* Champaign/Urbana, IL: National Council of Teachers of English.

Strum, P. (2010). *Westminster: School desegregation and Mexican-American rights.* Lawrence, KS: University Press of Kansas.

Willingham, D. (2009). *Why don't students like school? A cognitive scientist answers questions about how the mind works and what it means for the classroom.* New York, NY: Wiley Press and Antheneum.

Wirth, K., & Aziz, F. (2009). Better learning through better reading and reflecting. Retrieved from http:// serc.carleton.edu/acm_teagle/projects/wirth.html

Wray, A. (2002). *Formulaic language and the lexicon.* Cambridge, United Kingdom: Cambridge University Press.

Zwiers, J. (2005). Integrating academic language, thinking, and content: Learning scaffolds for non-native speakers in the middle grades. *Journal of English for Academic Purposes, 5,* 317–332.

## Appendix A: *Mendez v. Westminster: School Desegregation and Mexican-American Rights* (A Book Review)

Strum, P. (2010). *Westminster: School desegregation and Mexican-American rights*. Lawrence, KS: University Press of Kansas. (Nonfiction; 186 pages)

**Para 1:** While *Brown v. Board of Education* remains much more famous, *Mendez v. Westminster School District* (1947) was actually the first case in which segregation in education was successfully challenged in federal court. Finally giving Mendez its due, Philippa Strum provides a concise and compelling account of its legal issues and legacy, while retaining its essential human face: that of Mexican Americans unwilling to accept second-class citizenship.

**Para 2:** In 1945 Gonzalo and Felicitas Mendez, California farmers, sent their children off to the local school, only to be told that the youngsters would have to attend a separate facility reserved for Mexican Americans. In response the Mendezes and other aggrieved parents from nearby school districts went to federal court to challenge the segregation. Uniquely, they did not claim racial discrimination, since Mexicans were legally considered white, but rather discrimination based on ancestry and supposed "language deficiency" that denied their children their Fourteenth Amendment rights to equal protection under the law.

**Para 3:** Strum tells how, thanks to attorney David Marcus's carefully crafted arguments, federal district court judge Paul McCormick came to support the plaintiffs on the grounds that the social, psychological, and pedagogical costs of segregated education were damaging to Mexican-American children.

**Para 4:** The school districts claimed that federal courts had no jurisdiction over education, but the Ninth Circuit upheld McCormick's decision, ruling that the schools' actions violated California law. The appeal to the Ninth Circuit was supported by amicus briefs from leading civil liberties organizations, including the NAACP, which a few years later would adapt the arguments of Mendez in representing the plaintiffs in Brown.

**Para 5:** Strum effectively weaves together narrative and analysis with personality portraits to create a highly readable and accessible story, allowing us to hear the voices of all the protagonists. She also presents the issues evenhandedly, effectively balancing her presentation of arguments by both the plaintiffs and the schools that sought to continue the segregation of Mexican-American students.

**Para 6:** Ultimately, Mendez highlights how Mexican Americans took the lead to secure their civil rights and demonstrates how organization, courage, and persistence in the Mexican-American communities could overcome the racism of the school boards. Their inspiring example is particularly timely given the current controversies over immigration and the growing national interest in Latino life.

# Appendix B: *Angel Island: Gateway to Gold Mountain* (A Book Review)

From Partington, R. (2013, November). Angel Island. Retrieved from http://richiespicks.pbworks .com/w/page/67570942/angel%20island

Freedman, R. (2014). *Angel Island: Gateway to Gold Mountain.* New York, NY: Clarion.

**Para 1:** "It is said that these Chinese are entitled while they remain to the safeguards of the Constitution and to the protection of the laws in regard to their rights of person and of property, but that they continue to be aliens, subject to the absolute power of Congress to forcibly remove them. In other words, the guaranties of 'life, liberty, and property' named in the Constitution, are theirs by sufferance, and not of right. Of what avail are such guaranties? . . . In view of this enactment by the highest legislative body of the foremost Christian nation, may not the thoughtful Chinese disciple of Confucius fairly ask, 'Why do they send missionaries here?'"—from the 1893 dissenting opinion of U.S. Supreme Court Associate Justice David Brewer in Fong Yue Ting v. United States et al. Wong Quan v. United States et al. Lee Joe v. United States et al., in which the majority of the Court upheld the constitutionality of the Geary Act of 1892 (Retrieved from http:// supreme.justia.com/cases/federal/us/149/698/case.html)

**Para 2:** The Geary Act, as explained here by Russell Freedman, "required all persons of Chinese descent, including native-born citizens, to carry photo identification cards proving their lawful presence in the United States. At the time, no other group was required to hold such documents."

**Para 3:** That the Fong Yue Ting decision was handed down just three years prior to the Court's infamous Plessy v. Ferguson decision, has me suspecting that the late nineteenth century was a pretty lousy time to be anything but a white Christian male if you found yourself in America.

**Para 4:** And, yet, the willingness of the American Library Association's 1961 Newbery award committee to honor the Chinese stereotype-laden children's book, A CRICKET IN TIMES SQUARE (insuring the perpetuation of these stereotypes and prejudice through, yet, another generation thanks to all the teachers across the country who then read the ALA-blessed CRICKET to their elementary students), tells me that widespread acceptance of American anti-Chinese sentiment was not a passing fad, but was—and many might argue, still is—deeply entrenched. (Somewhere along the way, in later editions, the most egregious language in CRICKET was edited out.)

**Para 5:** Wait! I thought this was a book about Angel Island?

**Para 6:** And that it is. I learned from Freedman's ANGEL ISLAND: GATEWAY TO GOLD MOUNTAIN that the infamous immigration station on Angel Island, more than anything, was an important tool in decades-long, government-sanctioned, xenophobic legislating against Chinese immigrants and Chinese Americans trying to come home.

**Para 7:** That immigration station was built upon decades of prejudice: "Politicians . . . were demanding that Chinese immigrants be excluded from the United States. The Chinese were undesirable aliens, they charged, willing to take on any type of work and to work for longer hours for less pay—depriving whites of jobs. At a California Senate committee hearing in 1876, Chinese immigration was described as an 'unarmed invasion' that threatened the entire country. The rallying cry of the Workingmen's Party of California was 'The Chinese Must Go!'"

**Para 8:** (Doesn't that sound an awful lot like certain contemporary politicians and media darlings ranting about Hispanic immigrants and Hispanic Americans?)

**Para 9:** Here in California, ANGEL ISLAND: GATEWAY TO GOLD MOUNTAIN will be a welcome and important addition to the trade literature available to help teach California history.

**Para 10:** Freedman first walks readers through all of the atrocities perpetuated against the Chinese—by mobs and through legislation—beginning in the 1800s, so that when he proceeds to detail what Angel Island's Immigration Station was all about, we understand why the system there was set up as it was.

**Para 11:** We teach California history in fourth grade. Consistent with that fourth grade audience, this book is—in relation to Freedman's typical authorship—a relatively shorter book with relatively larger text and plenty of photos. It will be readily accessible to that fourth grade audience and will also serve quite notably as a great introduction for older readers who, like me, will likely finish it wanting to know more about all sorts of interrelated issues and events that Freedman introduces.

**Para 12:** It has now been five years since I rode the ferry from Tiburon over to Angel Island and wandered the trails around what is one heck of a beautiful place. Last time, it was the summer before the Immigration Station was opened as a museum. Now, understanding the significance of that facility, I'll be heading down there in the near future for another visit.

# Writing Arguments in World Languages: Scaffolding Content and Language Learning Simultaneously

*Pamela Spycher, WestEd*

*Thierry Spycher, Sacramento Unified School District*

High school students must develop the language and literacy skills necessary for success in college coursework, career environments, and meaningful engagement in civic life. Regardless of the choices young adults make in terms of the paths they will lead in their adult lives, in order to be informed and contributing members of society, all of them need to be able to develop deep understandings about complex topics, be critical consumers of media and other sources of knowledge, and know what constitutes sound evidence for claims that are made by various individuals and interest groups. They need to be independent thinkers, able to adapt to change in a rapidly evolving economy, and know how to generalize what they understand in one situation to new ones. All of these abilities require an advanced level of language and literacy skills that are drastically different from generations past, and it is increasingly unlikely that young people will find fulfilling and economically sustainable careers without them.

But the new era we are in requires much more than content knowledge and language and literacy skills applied independently. The jobs of today require people to collaborate effectively with others on work projects, understand how to engage others in meaningful conversations about issues that matter to them, and problem solve through collective thinking. To do this, young people also need to develop social and emotional skills related to collaborating. In our increasingly global society, this includes an appreciation and respect for diverse viewpoints and cultures, the willingness to engage with an open mind in conversations with others who might not share one's own viewpoints and culture, the confidence to hold one's ground with a cool head and strong evidence, and the self-awareness to know when there are gaps in understanding and how to reach out to others for guidance. All of these social and emotional skills are intertwined with language and literacy skills and deep understandings about disciplinary topics.

In this chapter, we address the use of the Common Core State Standards (CCSS; National Governors Association Center for Best Practices [NGA] & Council of Chief State School Officers [CCSSO], 2010) for literacy in integrated world language/social studies for ELLs and other culturally diverse learners in secondary settings. We'll start by discussing how the CCSS, integrated with the California World Language Content Standards (WLCS; California State Board of Education, 2010), present learning opportunities and demands in language, disciplinary literacy, and social studies content for ELLs and other linguistically diverse learners in high school. Next, we focus on the rationale for deciding how to meet the demands and enhance the potential of the CCSS and WLCS. The reasoning behind taking purposeful and intentional teaching approaches is driven by a cyclical process of inquiry ("What do my students need to be able to do, and where are they now?"), guided by sound theory and research ("How do people learn, and what has worked elsewhere to support learning?"), and anchored in tangible actions ("What specific approaches will support learning?"). We'll then focus on a pedagogical approach that supports students' achievement of the CCSS and WLCS, including some illustrative techniques that are useful for teachers across the disciplines in Grades 6–12. We'll conclude with some reflection questions and action plans useful for delving deeper into some of the ideas we discuss and trying out the teaching techniques we share.

## The Common Core State Standards and Specific Demands for ELLs

The CCSS offer a unique opportunity for creating more socially just educational environments and outcomes for ELLs and other culturally and linguistically diverse students. Implicit in the CCSS is a call for educational equity, as the overarching vision of the CCSS is for every student, by the time they graduate from high school, to be college and career ready and prepared for meaningful engagement with civic life. This focus is outlined in the capacities of literate individuals, which undergird the CCSS:

Students who are college and career ready...

- demonstrate independence;

- build strong content knowledge;

- respond to the varying demands of audience, task, purpose, and discipline;

- comprehend as well as critique;

- value evidence;

- use technology and digital media strategically and capably; and

- come to understand other perspectives and cultures. (NGA & CCSSO, 2010, p. 7)

However, while the vision of the CCSS—to ensure that all students develop full proficiency in each of these capacities across the disciplines—is a socially just one, the means by which to support all students to achieve this goal can often seem mysterious. The CCSS don't provide a roadmap. Creating one is a shared responsibility that includes teachers, teacher educators, leadership, policy makers, researchers, families and communities, and, of course, students themselves. Throughout this chapter, we tell the story of how we (Thierry and Pamela) worked collaboratively to create a pathway of progress toward the capacities of literate individuals for Thierry's high school students. Thierry is an experienced high school world languages (French) teacher working in a high poverty, culturally and linguistically diverse comprehensive public high school (Grades 9–12) in California. Although Thierry had been teaching French for more than a decade, Advanced Placement (AP) French was a new course for him. Pamela, a former classroom teacher, is an educational researcher interested in how best to support teachers to scaffold advanced disciplinary learning for culturally and linguistically diverse students. We'll share how Thierry integrated the CCSS into his existing practice. The impetus for doing so was not a state or district mandate, but, rather, a real professional need that he had to address: ensuring that each of his students could write evidence-based arguments in French.

Over half of the students in the high school where Thierry teaches are economically disadvantaged, and 80% are students of color (about 35% Latino, 30% Asian, 10% Black, and 10% multiracial). About half of the students in the school are classified as fluent English proficient, meaning that either they were at one time ELLs, or they entered school already proficient in English but speaking a language other than English at home. More than 22 languages other than English are spoken in these students' homes, mainly Spanish, Cantonese, Vietnamese, and Hmong. Thierry's AP French students featured in this chapter were seniors in their fourth year of learning French as an additional language and working toward achieving proficiency in the highest level, or Stage IV (Extended), of the WLCS.[1]

Just as other secondary content teachers do, world languages teachers must get to know their students—their cultural and linguistic backgrounds, prior academic experiences, social and emotional strengths and needs, and other aspects of their identities—in order to design instruction that works for individual students. Thierry's students brought a wealth of assets, including cultural and linguistic ones, to the classroom. At the same time, he recognized (and is told by students) that many also have academic language and literacy learning needs that have not yet been met through schooling, needs that do not magically disappear once his students walk through his classroom door.

Although Thierry was already using the WLCS to design instruction, which he found very useful, he felt that guidance on supporting his students with advanced disciplinary literacy was largely missing from these standards. When he started teaching AP French, he realized right away that the content of the AP French course was very demanding, requiring students to perform at high levels of competency in writing, speaking, listening, and reading in a wide array of content topics using only French. He wanted to make sure he was challenging his students in all aspects of

---

[1] The WLCS have four stages of cultural and linguistic proficiency (the language learning continuum). Proficiency in all stages along the language learning continuum are developed in five main categories— content, communication (interpersonal, interpretive, presentational), cultures, structures, and settings— which are intended to be integrated in instruction (California State Board of Education, 2010).

communication but also providing plenty of support for students to be successful with academic literacy, as not all students were confident writing a coherent and cohesive multiparagraph text, engaging in an extended conversation, interpreting a written or spoken text, or arguing from evidence in French.

The demands for academic literacy tasks *in French* that Thierry's AP French students face are similar to those that many other students, including ELLs, face with meeting the CCSS *in English* across the disciplines. We propose that when secondary teachers across the content areas use the CCSS in tandem with their content standards, students may experience a more coherent and fulfilling educational journey as they make their way toward the capacities of literate individuals. A brief look at the argument text writing standard for Grades 11–12 reveals how demanding the CCSS are. It also illustrates what we feel that most secondary teachers would like for their students to be able to do, regardless of content area.

## California CCSS Writing Standard 1, Grades 11–12

Write arguments to support claims in an analysis of substantive topics or texts, using valid reasoning and relevant and sufficient evidence.

  a. Introduce precise, knowledgeable claim(s), establish the significance of the claim(s), distinguish the claim(s) from alternate or opposing claims, and create an organization that logically sequences claim(s), counterclaims, reasons, and evidence.

  b. Develop claim(s) and counterclaims fairly and thoroughly, supplying the most relevant evidence for each while pointing out the strengths and limitations of both in a manner that anticipates the audience's knowledge level, concerns, values, and possible biases.

  c. Use words, phrases, and clauses as well as varied syntax to link the major sections of the text, create cohesion, and clarify the relationships between claim(s) and reasons, between reasons and evidence, and between claim(s) and counterclaims.

  d. Establish and maintain a formal style and objective tone while attending to the norms and conventions of the discipline in which they are writing.

  e. Provide a concluding statement or section that follows from and supports the argument presented.

  f. Use specific rhetorical devices to support assertions (e.g., appeal to logic through reasoning; appeal to emotion or ethical belief; relate a personal anecdote, case study, or analogy). (California State Board of Education, 2013)

The argument writing standard presents challenges for all students, but ELLs and other linguistically diverse students (who may not have access at home to the academic support needed to meet these demands) rely on their teachers for help achieving them. In this chapter, we'll share how, by focusing on both the WLCS and the CCSS and by implementing several highly interactive and scaffolded tasks that were anchored in complex texts, Thierry was in a better position to support his advanced world language students to meet these standards. Through these carefully designed learning tasks, his students became stronger at independently and critically reading complex texts, developed deep content knowledge of a globally relevant topic (women's rights), and made evidence-based claims in oral and written arguments in an academic register. Through instruction that integrated intellectually challenging content, an explicit focus on language, and scaffolded literacy tasks, his soon-to-be high school graduates developed both proficiency in and a greater sense of self-efficacy with the capacities of literate individuals.

## Rationale

As is the case in many secondary settings, a significant number of Thierry's students struggled with writing coherent and compelling arguments, which they needed to be able to do in order to be successful in his AP French class and on the AP French exam at the end of the year. Halfway through the first semester, the students were finishing a unit on the environment in which they had read and analyzed many articles on the subject, discussed their opinions about it, and even written short passages about it. At that point, Thierry felt that his students were ready to tackle the last assignment: writing an argumentative essay about the topic. All the students in the class were seniors, and about half of them had previously taken other AP classes and exams, so he was very surprised when one student asked him the following question: "*Monsieur, comment* écrit-*on une thèse d'un essai en français?* [Sir, how do you write a thesis statement for an argument in French?]" The obvious answer, to Thierry, was to tell this student that writing an argument in French isn't that different from writing an argument in English, thesis included. He felt certain that, by now, her senior year, she'd had lots of experience writing arguments. However, after he gave her this answer, she persisted: "*Mais, comment* écrit-*on une thèse d'un essai en français? Comment* écrit-*on une these?* [But, how do you write a thesis for an essay in French? How do you write a thesis?]"

This is when Thierry realized that, for this student, it wasn't so much that she didn't know how to write an argument in French. She didn't know how to write an argument. He soon realized that this student wasn't the only one. The following day, he asked his students to share their theses with one another so that he could see where the class was overall. They discussed the theses as a class, and, to his surprise, only one third of the students had a solid thesis. He knew that he was in trouble and had to come up with something to support his students. However, he'd had no preparation to do so. In his own words:

> Because I assumed that all my students would be able to apply their knowledge of writing an argument to the task of writing one in French, I was not prepared for students who did not know how to write an argument in the first place, and I had no resources or real practical answers to give them. The more I learned about teaching argumentative writing, the more I realized that I was facing of a monumental task. I started trying out different ways of teaching writing, but nothing was really working for my students.

When Thierry began learning more about the CCSS, he felt that they could provide him with guidance that would complement what he was already doing and support him to teach his students how to write an academic argument in French. More broadly, however, he recognized that if he could support his students to understand how to argue orally in French, analyze how French language arguments are written, and engage in scaffolded tasks intended to support them to write their own arguments in French, these understandings and skills could be transferred to their other classes and into college and careers. As Thierry began infusing the CCSS into his lessons, however, he very soon recognized that, as is the case with the WLCS, the CCSS focus on performance *outcomes* for students and not on what is needed to scaffold progress toward these outcomes.

It was at this point that Pamela, who was working with teachers in California on implementing the state's new English Language Development Standards (CA ELD Standards; California Department of Education, 2014) across the disciplines, shared with Thierry some of the approaches secondary content teachers were using to integrate the CA ELD Standards and the CCSS into disciplinary instruction. The CA ELD Standards focus on two main areas: "Interacting in Meaningful Ways" and "Learning About How English Works" (see Table 1 for an overview). In other words, they help teachers to focus their instructional attention on supporting ELLs to engage in collaborative academic conversations, interpret complex texts, and write increasingly complex texts themselves. At the same time, they help teachers support students to develop awareness about

## Table 1. The CA ELD Standards Overview

| Part I: Interacting in Meaningful Ways | Part II: Learning About How English Works |
|---|---|
| **A. Collaborative** (engagement in dialogue with others)<br>1. Exchanging information and ideas via oral communication and conversations<br>2. Interacting via written English (print and multimedia)<br>3. Offering opinions and negotiating with or persuading others<br>4. Adapting language choices to various contexts<br><br>**B. Interpretive** (comprehension and analysis of written and spoken texts)<br>5. Listening actively and asking or answering questions about what was heard<br>6. Reading closely and explaining interpretations and ideas from reading<br>7. Evaluating how well writers and speakers use language to present or support ideas<br>8. Analyzing how writers use vocabulary and other language resources<br><br>**C. Productive** (creation of oral presentations and written texts)<br>9. Expressing information and ideas in oral presentations<br>10. Writing literary and informational texts<br>11. Supporting opinions or justifying arguments and evaluating others' opinions or arguments<br>12. Selecting and applying varied and precise vocabulary and other language resources | **A. Structuring Cohesive Texts**<br>1. *Understanding text structure* and organization based on purpose, text type, and discipline<br>2. *Understanding cohesion* and how language resources across a text contribute to the way a text unfolds and flows<br><br>**B. Expanding and Enriching Ideas**<br>3. *Using verbs and verb phrases* to create precision and clarity in different text types<br>4. *Using nouns and noun phrases* to expand ideas and provide more detail<br>5. *Modifying to add details* to provide more information and create precision<br><br>**C. Connecting and Condensing Ideas**<br>6. *Connecting ideas* within sentences by combining clauses<br>7. *Condensing ideas* within sentences using a variety of language resources |

From California Department of Education. (2014). *California English language development standards*. Retrieved from http://www.cde.ca.gov/sp/el/er/eldstandards.asp

language itself and how to make intentional and deliberate choices with language in order to meet the expectations of different audiences. Another key element of the CA ELD Standards is that they focus heavily on scaffolding disciplinary language and literacy development in ways that maintain intellectual rigor (high levels of thinking and challenge with high levels of support).[2]

We bring the CA ELD Standards into the discussion here because, rather than being viewed as a separate set of standards, in California, these standards are seen as an integral part of CCSS implementation, and they are intended to be used to support ELLs' achievement of the CCSS and disciplinary learning across the content areas. Thierry saw value in leveraging what the CA ELD Standards have to offer and wanted to try out the instructional techniques derived from them as a way of scaffolding learning for his AP French students.

## Scaffolding Content and Language Learning Simultaneously

The pedagogical approaches we share in this chapter are grounded in the CCSS, WLCS, and CA ELD Standards, and they are derived from sociocultural and sociolinguistic theories of language and learning and the research that has emerged from these theories. Fundamentally, these theories view learning as a social process with scaffolding central to this process. Vygotsky (1978) proposed that people learn in their "zone of proximal development," the space that exists between what they can do independently and that which is too difficult for them to do without strategic support. More knowledgeable others (teachers and also other learners) play a key role in supporting learners to "stretch" to their next (or proximal) level of development. The term "scaffolding" refers to support for learners that is temporary and future oriented, that is, mindful of supporting learners to at some point become independent with particular tasks or understandings (Bruner, 1983; Walqui & van Lier, 2010). Scaffolding from teachers doesn't happen accidentally; teachers must know a lot about where their students are in the learning process so that they can plan learning tasks that help them progress toward a specified learning goal ("planned" scaffolding) and provide contingent support ("just-in-time" scaffolding) in the moment of teaching. Learning goals can be short term, such as a learning target for one lesson, or long term, such as outcome standards.

Another key conceptual framework that guided us was a transparent and explicit focus on language itself, a focus on language in the service of content learning (de Oliveira & Schleppegrell, 2015). When students understand how language works in complex disciplinary texts, they are in a better position to comprehend and critique what they are reading and effectively create their own advanced texts. For many secondary school students, particularly those who may not have access to academic language at home, this heightened awareness about language itself and how it is making meaning never materializes. An explicit focus on the language of complex texts in school—in all disciplines—plays a key role in disciplinary literacy instruction and, because it levels the playing field for many students, is a critical aspect of educational equity work. But how do we talk about language with our students?

Systemic functional linguistics (SFL) is a theory of language with practical pedagogical approaches that provide a way to demystify language and discuss it with students. SFL views

---

[2] More detailed guidance on how to do this is provided in California's new ELA/ELD Framework for K–12 schools. To access these free resources, visit the California Department of Education at www.cde.ca.gov.

language as a resource for making meaning and for getting things done in the world (not a set of rules to be memorized). This view of language helps teachers and students focus on the contexts in which language is used (including our purpose, or what we want to get done; the content and topic at hand; our audience; and mode of communication). Furthermore, SFL helps teachers and students to consider which language resources and language choices are most appropriate for which contexts (Christie & Derewianka, 2008; Halliday, 1993; Schleppegrell, 2004). For example, what kind of language would be most appropriate when explaining to a young child why mommy got a speeding ticket? How would our language choices change if we were explaining the speeding ticket to a traffic court judge, or talking about it at a cocktail party?

These register choices, and how to make them, can be learned in the classroom through scaffolded analysis of what language is doing in different contexts and in texts, along with lots of practice using (or "trying on") new language that has been discovered and discussed. SFL-derived pedagogy offers a way for teachers and students to discuss the language of the complex texts that are critical for disciplinary content learning in ways that a) support students to understand the content meanings of the text better and b) empower students to make more informed language choices when they produce their own spoken or written texts. A growing body of studies in secondary settings the United States has demonstrated how this language-rich focus on content results in improved academic outcomes for culturally and linguistically diverse students, including EL students (see, e.g., de Oliveira, 2010; Schleppegrell & O'Hallaron, 2011; Spycher, 2007). In the next section, we'll share some of the approaches that Thierry used in his classroom that integrate the WLCS, CCSS, and CA ELD Standards and that draw upon SFL and other sociocultural/sociolinguistic theories and research.

## Pedagogical Practice: Teaching and Learning Cycle

The unit from which we will show examples focused on global women's rights. Learning targets for individual lessons varied, but the culminating task for the unit was for students to be able to write an evidence-based written argument about the progress of women's rights globally. In order to reach this goal, Thierry planned many interactive tasks where students engaged in collaborative conversations, analytical reading, daily writing, and language analysis, all in an integrated way. The WLCS and CCSS that Thierry used to guide his planning of the unit are listed in Table 2. Thierry also used the CA ELD Standards in instructional planning in order to scaffold content and language learning.

To frame the various interactive and collaborative tasks in which his students would be engaging and to ensure that he provided his students with the scaffolding they would need to successfully write arguments in French, Thierry used the "teaching and learning cycle" (Figure 1), which we adapted from previous SFL-derived research (including de Oliveira & Lan, 2014; de Oliveira, Klassen, & Maune, 2015; Derewianka & Jones, 2012; Gibbons, 2015; Rose & Martin, 2012; Spycher, 2007; Spycher & Linn-Nieves, 2014). In the teaching and learning cycle, teachers guide their students through four phases of learning: (1) building content knowledge through language rich experiences, (2) learning about the language of text type, (3) jointly constructing texts, and (4) constructing texts independently.

## Table 2. WLCS and CCSS in Action in the Women's Rights Unit

| World Language Content Standards, Stage IV (Extended) | California Common Core State Standards, Grades 11–12 |
|---|---|
| **Content**<br>4.0. Students acquire information, recognize distinctive viewpoints, and further their knowledge of other disciplines.<br>4.1. Students address complex, concrete, factual, and abstract topics related to the immediate and external environment, including societal expectations . . . social and political issues, belief systems . . .<br><br>**Communication**<br>4.0. Students use extended language (coherent and cohesive multi-paragraph texts).<br>4.1. Engage in oral, written, or signed (ASL) conversations.<br>4.2. Interpret written, spoken, or signed (ASL) language.<br>4.3. Present to an audience of listeners, readers, or ASL viewers.<br>4.4. Discuss, compare and contrast, and support an opinion; persuade.<br>4.5. Demonstrate understanding of the main ideas and most details in authentic texts.<br>4.6. Produce and present a complex written, oral, or signed (ASL) product in a culturally authentic way.<br><br>**Cultures**<br>4.2. Explain similarities and differences in the target cultures and between students' own cultures.<br>4.3. Explain the changes in perspectives when cultures come in contact.<br><br>**Structures**<br>4.0. Students use knowledge of extended discourse to understand abstract and academic topics.<br>4.1. Use extended discourse (native-like text structure) to produce formal communications.<br>4.2. Identify similarities and differences in the extended discourse (native-like text structure) of the languages the students know.<br><br>**Settings**<br>4.0. Students use language in informal and formal settings. | **Reading Informational Text**<br>RI.11–12.7. Integrate and evaluate multiple sources of information presented in different media or formats (e.g., visually, quantitatively) as well as in words in order to address a question or solve a problem.<br><br>**Speaking and Listening**<br>SL.11–12.1. Initiate and participate effectively in a range of collaborative discussions (one-on-one, in groups, and teacher-led) with diverse partners on grades 11–12 topics, texts, and issues, building on others' ideas and expressing their own clearly and persuasively . . .<br><br>**Writing**<br>W.11–12.1. Write arguments to support claims in an analysis of substantive topics or texts, using valid reasoning and relevant and sufficient evidence . . .<br>W.11–12.4. Produce clear and coherent writing in which the development, organization, and style are appropriate to task, purpose, and audience.<br><br>**Language**<br>L.11–12.3. Apply knowledge of language to understand how language functions in different contexts, to make effective choices for meaning or style, and to comprehend more fully when reading or listening. |

From California State Board of Education. (2010). *World Language Content Standards for California Public Schools: Kindergarten Through Grade Twelve*. Retrieved from http://www.cde.ca.gov/be/st/ss/documents/worldlanguage2009.pdf and California State Board of Education. (2013). *California Common Core State Standards: English Language Arts and Literacy in History/Social Studies, Science, and Technical Subjects*. Sacramento: California Department of Education. Retrieved from http://www.cde.ca.gov/be/st/ss/documents/finalelaccssstandards.pdf

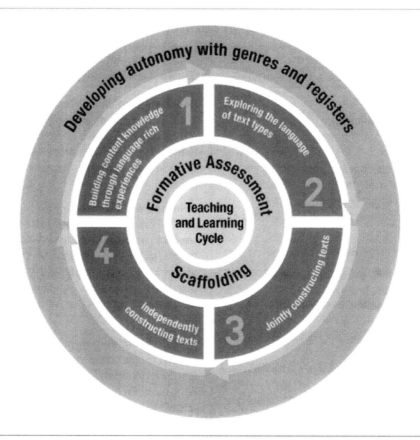

*Figure 1. The Teaching and Learning Cycle*

The advantage of using this type of unit framing is that it focuses teachers' attention on the phases, or "big buckets," of student learning in a way that makes it impossible to neglect scaffolding. Progress through these phases occurs over many days or weeks (not in one or two lessons). Important to note is that while phase 1 (building content knowledge through language-rich experiences) begins the cycle, building content knowledge continues in tandem with each of the other phases throughout the life of the unit. Next, we'll share some examples of approaches Thierry used in each phase and how scaffolding came into play in each one.

## Phase 1: Building Content Knowledge Through Language-Rich Experiences

As a world languages teacher, Thierry's students were already verbally interacting a lot—in conversations, short dialogs, oral presentations, and other oral exchanges—but his new challenge with his AP French class was to raise the intellectual rigor of these collaborative conversations, anchoring them in complex texts and focusing on building not only advanced French language proficiency, but also deep content knowledge through the language of French. One of the approaches that Thierry tried out in this phase was "expert group jigsaw" with complex texts (see Figure 2). Expert group jigsaw is largely a reading comprehension task, as it supports students as they delve deeply into a complex text and forces them to talk about it. Through the discussion about the reading, guided by strategically-designed focus questions and a structured process, students deepen their understanding of the text's content while they simultaneously strengthen their

## Expert Group Jigsaw Procedure

In this approach, the students are doing the work. The teacher's job starts with setting things up ahead of time through "planned scaffolding" (by choosing texts worthy of reading and discussing, deciding how to group students, determining how much time students will need for each step, preparing the note-taking guide, etc.). During the lesson, the teacher observes students closely as they interact in order to provide "just-in-time" scaffolding (clarifying, asking probing questions, etc.) and determine how students are processing the information and interacting with their peers.

### Step 1: Students read a text independently in their expert groups
The expert groups convene. Sometimes, groups can be put together randomly (by counting off, for example). At other times, teachers may want to group students strategically in order to balance/leverage strengths, learning needs, and interests. Each person in the same expert group reads the same text, but each of the different expert groups read a different text. This could be different sections from the same text, or it could be different texts that provide various lenses on the same topic. Each student reads his or her text independently, along with focus questions and a note-taking guide (graphic organizer) to take notes.

### Step 2: Students become experts in their expert groups
In this step, each person is responsible for adding information from their independent reading, noting (in their note-taking guide) what others share, and building on what has been shared. After the initial sharing, the students move on to discussion questions about the text where they can delve deeper into the text together and further develop their expertise of the topic. At the end of this phase, the group members agree on key points they will each share in their jigsaw groups.

### Step 3: Students share their expertise and learn from others in jigsaw groups
Students convene in their jigsaw groups, composed of one (or two) people from each expert group. Each person shares their expertise while the others take notes and ask clarification or elaboration questions. Once each person has shared, the group may have an additional task, such as synthesizing the information that has been shared or discussing one or more of the big ideas from the different readings.

### Step 4: Students share what they learned in their expert groups
Students reconvene in their expert groups and share what they each learned from their different jigsaw groups. Each person adds any new information to their note-taking guide and makes connections, asks questions, builds on ideas, etc.

*Figure 2. Expert Group Jigsaw*

reading, speaking, listening, and writing skills. It is during the text-based discussion that reading comprehension blossoms.

When Thierry's students engaged in the expert group jigsaw, each expert group read different texts (in French) on the status of women's rights globally. For example, one expert group read an article about how, from the perspective of the author, women's rights have stalled and even regressed in some parts of the Arab world. Another group read about how women's rights in France have progressed dramatically over the past century. When the groups convened to discuss their reading selections, they were motivated to discuss them, partly because the topic was relevant to them as emerging adults and partly because they were curious to find out what their peers learned and thought. Naturally, they were also eager to share their own perspectives (see Figure 3).

Expert group jigsaw is an effective approach because it is supportive, inclusive, and equitable. The approach is most effective when the expert groups have a) a structured process, such as an assigned group facilitator and time-keeper, so that all students are obliged to engage in the

*Figure 3. Students Interacting During Expert Group Jigsaw*

conversation and stay on track with time limits; b) focus questions that focus their attention on what's important in the text; and c) a graphic organizer that guides their reading, centers their text-based conversation, and holds each person accountable for contributing something. The technique is quite flexible, and there are many variations to the process we're sharing. Unfortunately, in our experience, the approach is severely underused in content instruction, which is a shame because its use results in deeper learning for students and a more positive classroom climate.

## Phase 2: Learning About the Language of Text Types

Once his students had some foundational understandings about women's rights globally (through many reading and discussion tasks, including expert group jigsaw), they were ready to learn more about the language of the text type: argumentative essays. For this phase, Thierry tried out another highly interactive approach, "text reconstruction" (see Figure 4). During this activity, students just listen to a very short "mentor" text as the teacher reads it aloud, then take notes as the text is read aloud a second and third time, and finally work collaboratively with a partner or small group to reconstruct the text as closely as they can to the original. After that, the teacher draws their attention to particular language the author used and to the overall structure of the text so that the students have explicit understanding of what type of language is used in this text type and how that language conveys meaning. The overarching purpose of this approach (and of all language work) is to deepen content knowledge, as students must negotiate the meaning of the text they reconstruct during the activity (because it has to make sense). An additional key purpose is to "apprentice" students into the writing of a particular text type by scaffolding their reconstruction of it with multiple opportunities to hear it, their notes, and the support of their peers.

**Text Reconstruction Procedure**

In this approach, it's important to select (or write) a short text ahead of time, one that includes the content and language that students will be "apprenticed" to use. Students are doing most of the work here, and the teacher's job is to observe them closely as they interact, providing "just-in-time" scaffolding when needed and to determine which content ideas and language features should be delved into after the activity (step 6 and beyond).

1. **Focused Listening:** Teacher reads a short text (60 seconds or less to read aloud) that models the text type (e.g., argument) students are reading and will later be writing. Teacher focuses the listening by asking the students to listen for words or phrases critical to the content. Students just listen (no writing yet).

2. **Simple Note-Taking:** Teacher reads the text a second time while students take notes consisting of key words critical to the content.

3. **Extended Note-Taking (optional):** Teacher reads the text a third and final time while students take additional notes, focusing on phrases and longer strings of words critical to the content and also for cohesion (e.g., text connectives, time phrases).

4. **Oral Reconstruction:** Students (in partners) take turns sharing their notes with one another, essentially orally reconstructing the text. Each listener adds notes they don't already have as they listen to their partner.

5. **Written Reconstruction:** Students (in same partners or in groups of four) work collaboratively to reconstruct the text in writing. Their goal is to reconstruct the text as closely as they can to the original, using their notes as a scaffold.

6. **Focused Attention to Language:** A volunteer shares their reconstructed text on the document reader while the other students look for differences and similarities in their own texts. Then teacher shows the original text and points out key language features s/he wants them to focus as they progress in their own argument writing (e.g., content vocabulary, persuasive language, text connectives, complex sentences).

*Figure 4. Text Reconstruction*

Adapted from Gibbons (2015) and Spycher & Linn-Nieves (2014).

When Thierry tried out this approach in the women's rights unit, he chose a mentor text that would focus his students' attention on an opening paragraph of an argument, which includes the thesis statement:

Original text in French:

*Largement défavorisée à travers les siècles précédents, aujourd'hui la femme voit son statut évoluer. En effet, avec cette abondance de nouveaux droits depuis le droit de vote qui leur est accordé en 1944 et leur permettant de défendre aussi bien leur vie professionnelle que privée, on constate l'apparition d'un nouveau type de femme: la femme égalitaire qui s'oppose dorénavant à la femme strictement menagerie. (Dissertation de Français sur les droits des femmes, 2010)*

Our translation:

*Widely disadvantaged through previous centuries, today women are seeing their status evolve. Indeed, with the abundance of new rights since the right to vote was granted to them in 1944, permitting them to defend both their professional and private lives, we see the emergence of a new type of woman: the egalitarian woman who henceforth strictly opposes the housewife.*

One of Thierry's goals in selecting this particular text was for his students to see a model of a strong opening paragraph with a solid thesis statement, one they could discuss and grapple with as they reconstructed the paragraph. The specific language features he wanted to draw their attention to were the academic vocabulary and stance used. He also wanted to draw their attention to how the paragraph starts with an adverbial phrase ("Widely disadvantaged through previous centuries . . ."), which "sets the scene" but can also be confusing to students because it is so densely packed with information and has a structure that is typical of academic texts in French, which may be unfamiliar to students who have only been learning the language for a few years. Text reconstruction gave him an opportunity to unpack some of this language with his students after they'd done some grappling with it themselves. Examples of one student's notes (steps 2 and 3) and reconstructed text (step 5) are shown in Figures 5 and 6.

One outcome that we found interesting, as we viewed video of students engaging in the task, is that as students were negotiating the meanings of the text and discussing how to put language together to reconstruct these meanings, they were not just using academic French (in both speaking and writing) in new and meaningful ways. They were also engaging effectively in a collaborative conversation in French using the appropriate register for that communicative task, including building on others' ideas and expressing their own ideas clearly and persuasively.

## Phase 3: Jointly Constructing Texts

By this point, Thierry's students had engaged in many interactive reading, writing, speaking, listening, and language analysis tasks, all in the service of understanding the topic better and developing

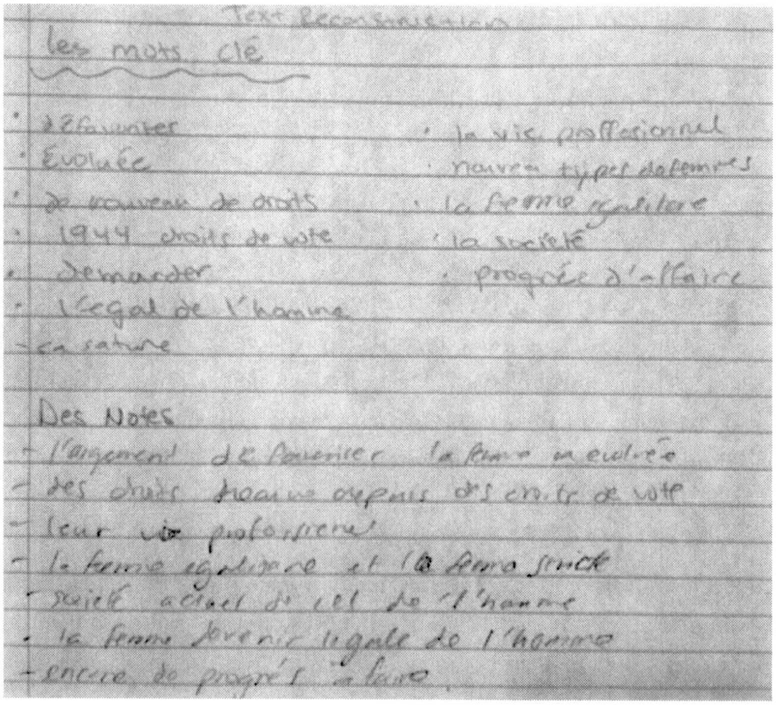

*Figure 5. Student's Notes During Collaborative Text Reconstruction*

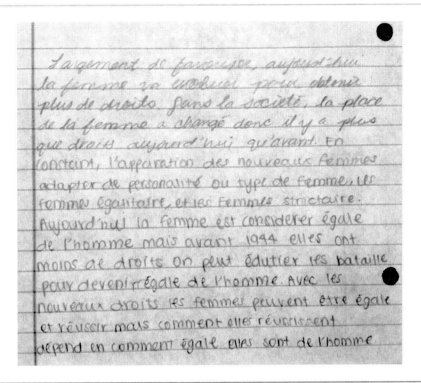

*Figure 6. Student's Reconstructed Text During Text Reconstruction*

proficiency in writing arguments. Before Thierry asked his students to write their own arguments on the topic, he wanted to try out another approach that would prepare them for independent writing. When "jointly constructing texts," the teacher's role is to write, facilitating students' oral construction of the text while guiding them to improve the text as they are coconstructing it (and not just scribing what the students say). The idea is to scaffold students' writing while also providing an opportunity for them to express their content understandings (sometimes, just saying content ideas aloud helps to clarify them). When jointly constructing texts with students, teachers might prompt them to add details to their sentences to expand or enrich them; elaborate on their thinking; reshape the text by moving or crossing out words, phrases, or whole sentences; add text connectives for cohesion; use more precise vocabulary; or condense their ideas by combining clauses or through nominalization.[3] These are just some of the things teachers can do to scaffold writing at this phase.

When Thierry jointly constructed the first paragraph of an argument with his class, he wrote on the document reader while the students did most of the talking—contributing their ideas, agreeing or disagreeing, adding details or suggestions for refinement. As the text was coconstructed, it was simultaneously being revised and edited, and the "final" version was marked up with lots of crossed-out text, words added to sentences, and circled sentences that needed to be moved to

---

[3] Nominalization is the grammatical process of creating a noun or noun phrase from another part of speech or condensing large amounts of information (e.g., an event or concept) into a noun or noun phrase. For example, "It rained a lot all over the place" can be nominalized into "widespread flooding."

another place in the text. Once this work was done, each student wrote the final, coconstructed paragraph in their own notebooks so that they'd have another mentor text to refer to when they wrote their own argument texts.

## Phase 4: Constructing Texts Independently

In our experience, what typically happens in classrooms (and what we have done a lot of ourselves) is that teachers spend a lot of time on rich content learning—reading lots of different texts, writing notes, discussing important topics, viewing videos, and so on—and then jump straight to asking students to write an argument (or explanation, information report, etc.). What we are proposing is that more scaffolding is needed for students to be able to independently construct effective texts. Teachers can use the teaching and learning cycle to a) continue all of those effective approaches for content knowledge building and perhaps refine them with more scaffolding for language learners (phase 1 of the cycle) and also b) scaffold students' language awareness and capacities to use language effectively by giving them plenty of time to discuss, analyze, and experiment/play with language (phases 2 and 3). By the time Thierry's students reached phase 4 of the teaching and learning cycle, they were confident and prepared to write their own successful argument texts in French. They can now carry these understandings about argument texts to their other academic content classes and into their adult lives.

## Concluding Thoughts

In this chapter, we've provided some examples of how teachers might use the teaching and learning cycle to organize and plan instruction that promotes students' growth in disciplinary literacy and their advancement along the language development continuum. The learning tasks we featured are by no means the only ones that teachers can use at each phase of the teaching and learning cycle. Rather, they are illustrative of how teachers might sequence lessons in a coherent way; plan lessons that integrate reading, writing, speaking, listening, and language; draw students' attention to how language works in different disciplines and in various text types; and support simultaneous content and language learning through collaborative group work around complex texts. Whichever learning tasks teachers choose to use along the teaching and learning cycle, all tasks must be purposeful and carefully designed to build toward what we ultimately want our students to be able to do, including making arguments that are well-supported by claims. The learning tasks are the means to an end, and not an end in themselves.

Integrating three sets of standards (the WLCS, CCSS, and CA ELD Standards) might feel like a daunting proposition. For Thierry, the key was to gradually "layer in" new learning to what he was already doing. Also, he chose to think of it not as three distinct sets of standards but, rather, three tools or lenses that complemented one another to strengthen his instructional practice. Like most teachers we know, he is always looking for ways to strengthen and refine his practice because he wants all of his students to be successful with the intellectually rich, academically challenging tasks in his courses and have desirable options for their futures, including college, careers, and meaningful engagement with civic life. Without developing the capacities of literate individuals, these options are limited. Thierry took some risks by trying out several new approaches, and the risks paid off for his students. It was no accident that the tasks he had students engage in were designed for learning through social interaction and that the texts he selected were both intellectually challenging and highly relevant for students on the cusp of adulthood. Learning—at all ages—should feel like it's worth the effort and (yes, we'll say it) even fun!

## Reflection Questions and Action Plans

### Reflection Questions

1. Which approaches from this chapter are similar to what you are already doing in your instructional practice? Is there anything you might want to refine, based on what you learned here?

2. Which approach would you like to try out with your own students? What would you like to accomplish by implementing this approach? What is your first step?

3. How might a greater focus on meaningful interaction and learning about how language works support your students to succeed in your content-area classes?

4. How might using the CCSS and your state's ELD standards in your instructional planning support your ELLs and other linguistically diverse students to develop disciplinary literacy in your content area?

### Action Plans

1. Take another look at a unit or lesson you have already implemented (and like). Add in one of the approaches from this chapter. Observe your students carefully to see what happens.

2. Try one new way of supporting students to engage in a collaborative conversation anchored in complex text. Ask them how they liked it and what they learned.

3. Try talking about language with your students once a week in each class, and see what happens. Ask your students what they think about it.

4. Ready to learn more? Take a look at some of the resources we use, which you can find in the References section. Choose one text to delve more deeply into with a colleague, and try out some of the approaches.

## References

Bruner, J. S. (1983). *Child's talk: Learning to use language*. New York, NY: Norton.

California Department of Education. (2014). *California English language development standards*. Sacramento, CA: Author. Retrieved from http://www.cde.ca.gov/sp/el/er/eldstandards.asp

California State Board of Education. (2010). *World language content standards for California public schools: Kindergarten through grade twelve*. Sacramento, CA: Author. Retrieved from http://www.cde.ca.gov/be/st/ss/documents/worldlanguage2009.pdf

California State Board of Education. (2013). *California Common Core State Standards: English language arts and literacy in history/social studies, science, and technical subjects*. Sacramento, CA: Author. Retrieved from http://www.cde.ca.gov/be/st/ss/documents/finalelaccssstandards.pdf

Christie, F., & Derewianka, B. (2008). *School discourse: Learning to write across the years of schooling*. London, United Kingdom: Continuum.

de Oliveira, L. C. (2010). Nouns in history: Packaging information, expanding explanations, and structuring reasoning. *The History Teacher, 43*(2), 191–203.

de Oliveira, L. C., Klassen, M., & Maune, M. (2015). From detailed reading to independent writing: Scaffolding instruction for ELLs through knowledge about language. In L. C. de Oliveira, M. Klassen, & M. Maune (Eds.), *The Common Core State Standards in English language arts for English language learners: Grades 6–12* (pp. 65–77). Alexandria, VA: TESOL Press.

de Oliveira, L. C., & Lan, S-W. (2014). Writing science in an upper elementary classroom: A genre-based approach to teaching English language learners. *Journal of Second Language Writing, 25*(1), 23–39.

de Oliveira, L. C., & Schleppegrell, M. J. (2015). *Focus on grammar and meaning.* Oxford, United Kingdom: Oxford University Press.

Derewianka, B., & Jones, P. (2012). *Teaching language in context.* Melbourne, Australia: Oxford University Press.

Dissertation de Français sur les droits des femmes. (2010, September 18). Retrieved from http://www.devoir-de -philosophie.com/dissertation-dissertation-francais-sur-droits-des-femmes-31181.html

Gibbons, P. (2015). *Scaffolding language, scaffolding learning.* Portsmouth, NH: Heinemann.

Halliday, M. A. K. (1993). Toward a language-based theory of education. *Linguistics and Education 5,* 93–116.

National Governors' Association Center for Best Practices & Council of Chief State School Officers. (2010). *Common Core State Standards for English language arts and literacy in history/social studies, science, and technical subjects.* Washington, DC: Authors. http://www.corestandards.org

Rose, D., & Martin, J. R. (2012). *Learning to write, reading to learn; genre, knowledge and pedagogy in the Sydney school.* London, England: Equinox.

Schleppegrell, M. J., & O'Hallaron, C. L. (2011). Teaching academic language in L2 secondary settings. *Annual Review of Applied Linguistics, 31,* 3–18.

Spycher, P. (2007). Academic writing of adolescent English learners: Learning to use "although." *Journal of Second Language Writing, 16*(4), 238–254.

Spycher, P., & Linn-Nieves, K. (2014). Reconstructing, deconstructing, and constructing complex texts. In P. Spycher (Ed.), *The Common Core State Standards in English language arts/literacy for English language learners: Grades K–5.* Alexandria, VA: TESOL Press.

Vygotsky, L. S. (1978). *Mind in society: The development of higher psychological processes.* Cambridge, United Kingdom: Cambridge University Press.

Walqui, A., & van Lier, L. (2010). *Scaffolding the academic success of adolescent English language learners: A pedagogy of promise.* San Francisco, CA: WestEd.

# Conclusion

*Luciana C. de Oliveira*

The mission of the Common Core State Standards (CCSS; National Governors Association Center for Best Practices [NGA] & Council of Chief State School Officers [CCSSO], 2010) is to prepare students for college and career readiness. The standards show what is to be learned at each grade level, from Grades K–12. The standards "define what all students are expected to know and be able to do, not how teachers should teach" (NGA & CCSSO, 2010, p. 6). It is up to school districts, schools, and especially teachers to develop curricula that align with the CCSS. Teachers are responsible for structuring units of instruction to support all students. In addition, with little guidance provided by the CCSS to support ELLs, teachers have the additional task of developing curriculum that is appropriate for the needs of this student population. The chapters in this volume provide ideas for teachers to focus their instruction on crucial aspects of the content areas of history/ social studies and science, and ideas for how to integrate several content areas and address literacy instruction to support ELLs so they can be successful in school and beyond.

Teachers need to have a clear understanding about aspects of content-area instruction that can best support language development for their ELLs, but also need to consider the language resources their students bring to the classroom and build from what students know, because ELLs need to develop their language and literacy repertoires from what they know. This requires teachers to think about language in ways that consider ELLs' backgrounds and experiences and the expectations and demands of the CCSS for literacy. Teachers who understand how to facilitate learning experiences in which their ELLs engage deeply with multimodal texts and tasks are in a better position to help them develop their linguistic and academic repertoires.

The CCSS in English language arts and literacy are supposed to prepare students not only to be more literate individuals but to participate in the world:

> The skills and knowledge captured in the ELA/literacy standards are designed to prepare students for life outside the classroom. They include critical-thinking skills and the ability to closely and attentively read texts in a way that will help them understand and enjoy complex works of literature. Students will learn to use cogent reasoning and evidence collection skills that are essential for success in college, career, and life. The standards also lay out a vision of what it means to be a literate person who is prepared for success in the 21st century. (NGA & CCSSO, 2014)

This volume, along with the other volumes in the series, asks educators to consider the content and language demands of the CCSS for ELLs, and provide specific pedagogical practices, strategies, and ideas for teachers to reflect on the kind of instruction that is possible for making the demands of language use explicit. I hope this book is a useful resource for teachers to improve their instruction by considering the demands of the CCSS for their students and implementing strategies that address these demands.

## References

National Governors Association Center for Best Practices & Council of Chief State School Officers. (2010). *Common Core State Standards for English language arts & literacy in history/social studies, science & technical subjects*. Washington, DC: Authors. Retrieved from http://www.corestandards.org/wp-content/uploads/ELA_Standards.pdf

National Governors Association Center for Best Practices & Council of Chief State School Officers. (2014). *English language arts standards*. Retrieved from http://www.corestandards.org/ELA-Literacy/